LOCAL GOVERNMENT IN WALES

ITS ROLE AND FUNCTIONS

**George A Boyne   Paul Griffiths
Alan Lawton   Jennifer Law**

JOSEPH
ROWNTREE
FOUNDATION

Published by the
Joseph Rowntree Foundation
The Homestead
40 Water End
York YO3 6LP

Tel: (0904) 629241

ISBN 1 872470 43 2

Design and setting by Peter Adkins Design Co.

Printed in Great Britain by Maxiprint, York

The authors are researchers at the Welsh Unit for Local Government, Polytechnic of Wales

CONTENTS

PREFACE

This research, commissioned by the Joseph Rowntree Foundation, provides the first comprehensive analysis of local government in Wales. The empirical work was undertaken from April to December 1990, and the report was written during the first few months of 1991. Throughout the project the environment of local government was especially turbulent. A decade of frequent and substantial policy change culminated in the introduction of the poll tax in April 1990. By the time our study had been completed the Conservative government had decided to reform local taxation again and had outlined plans for a new structure of local government based on unitary authorities.

We are grateful that, despite being condemned to live in such turbulent times, many officials in local authorities and the Welsh Office were prepared to assist our research. The information, insight and advice which they provided have been invaluable. We are also grateful to the members of the Joseph Rowntree Foundation advisory group who commented on a draft of our report, and to Peter John who gave helpful guidance on the general direction of our work. Any remaining errors of fact or interpretation are our collective responsibility.

George A Boyne
Paul Griffiths
Alan Lawton
Jennifer Law
Welsh Unit for Local Government,
Polytechnic of Wales, April 1991

CHAPTER 1

AIMS AND METHODS

THE BROAD AIM of this project reflects the research brief provided by the Joseph Rowntree Foundation: to analyse the role and functions of local government in Wales.

In contrast to the situation in England, there is little previous research that serves as a basis for the analysis of local government in Wales. In order to provide the required depth of analysis it has therefore been necessary to undertake a substantial amount of new empirical work and to focus on the following key issues contained in the research brief: the distinctive functions of Welsh local authorities; changes in the role of local authorities since 1974; local autonomy and discretion; geographical variations in the content and methods of service delivery; the structure of the local government system and the scale of individual units. These issues are addressed in Chapters 2 to 6 of the report.

The aim of Chapter 2 is to establish whether there is a separate local government system in Wales. Most discussions of local government treat England and Wales as a single system. We analyse the historical and political context of Welsh local government, the role of the Welsh Office, the pattern of central-local relations and the growth of policy communities that deal with local government issues. We survey the circulars to local authorities issued by the Welsh Office, and compare the spending and central funding of Welsh councils with councils in English non-metropolitan areas. An empirical analysis is conducted to identify whether the high grants received by Welsh councils are simply the product of their high needs and low resources, or the product of a funding framework that is more generous than that enjoyed by their English counterparts. The conclusion of Chapter 2 is that there is a separate Welsh local government system which is distinguished by its institutional structure, its processes of central-local relations, and its pattern of local policies.

The aim of Chapter 3 is to identify the impact of central constraints on local autonomy in Wales. It is widely believed that local authorities have suffered an unprecedented decline in their autonomy since the 1970s. Our analysis of this issue is in three stages. First, we identify the main policy objectives of central government. Second, we analyse empirically whether these central objectives have been achieved. This involves an examination of trends since 1974 in the aggregate level of current and capital spending, the quantity of direct service provision and the use of market criteria of resource allocation. We also assess whether local policy diversity has declined over time, with particular reference to local compliance with central spending targets, the extent of local variations in service provision, and the strength of the link between party control and redistributive policies. The third stage of our analysis is concerned with the impact of central government on the level of uniformity of the provision of different services. Why, for example, is the provision of education highly uniform while the provision of cultural facilities is highly variable? The overall conclusion of Chapter 3 is that while central government has achieved some of its policy objectives, the extent of the decline in local autonomy has been exaggerated.

The aim of Chapter 4 is to provide a 'map' of the current role of local authorities in the delivery of services. To what extent have Welsh councils moved away from a traditional role of direct service provision towards an 'enabling' role of facilitating and regulating service provision by other organisations? Our analysis of this issue is based on an extensive questionnaire survey of chief executives in both county and district councils, education officers in the counties and housing officers in the districts. In addition over 40 interviews were conducted with officials in the Welsh Office and local authority officers throughout Wales. Our research indicates that styles of service provision differ both across local areas and within individual authorities. There has been some movement towards an enabling role, partly as a response to central pressures and partly as a pragmatic response to local circumstances. However, the conclusion of Chapter 4 is that direct provision remains the dominant role, and that this is the role which most Welsh councils would prefer to retain.

The aim of Chapter 5 is to evaluate recent proposals for the reform of local government in Wales. The government, the opposition parties and the local authority associations have all argued that reform is required. We summarise their arguments and prescriptions, and then use the criteria of 'democracy' and 'functional performance' to evaluate the reform proposals. The agenda for reform in Wales consists largely of the issues of structure (one or two major tiers) and scale (population size and geographical area). We argue that the values of democracy and functional performance are best promoted by a local government system which has the following characteristics: more than one tier of authorities, small-scale authorities, and scope for diversity in both structure and scale in order to reflect local preferences and circumstances. The conclusion of Chapter 5 is that no one set of reform proposals embraces all of these characteristics, but that there are elements in each set which could be combined to form the basis of a better local government system.

Finally in Chapter 6 we consider the implications of our research for the future role and functions of local government in Wales.

CHAPTER 2

THE DISTINCTIVE CHARACTERISTICS OF WELSH LOCAL GOVERNMENT

A STUDENT OF British public administration who relied on academic literature might never become aware of the existence of Welsh local government, let alone its distinctive characteristics. The literature on local government may occasionally use the phrase "England and Wales" but will then proceed to discuss only England on the presumption that Wales must be the same. The literature on Welsh politics and Welsh history makes very little reference to the structures, processes and outputs of Welsh local government. Perhaps, in part mitigation for this gap in Welsh academic concern, the case for a separate study of Welsh local government rests largely on the circumstances of the late twentieth century. Until recent years, the local administration and the local government of Wales lay within a structure identical to that of England.

The aim of this chapter is to identify the distinguishing characteristics of the Welsh local government system. Part I outlines the historical development and distinctive political setting of local authorities in Wales. Part II examines the structure of local government and the processes of central-local relations. Part III analyses the outputs of the Welsh local government system, with particular emphasis on legislation, circulars, grants and spending. Part IV summarises the distinctive features of local government in Wales.

I Historical development and political context
a) Historical development
The Acts of Union (1536-43) were designed to placate the conquered territories of Wales by awarding them the constitutional system of England. The state administration of Tudor England was imposed on Wales through the designation of

13 county boundaries (Williams, 1985). These same boundaries were to remain the structure for local administration and then local government until 1974.

The Local Government Acts of 1888 and 1894 were designed to transform the increasingly complex structures of local administration into a system of democratic local government. The Acts applied equally to Wales and England. The 1888 Act created directly elected County Councils responsible initially for the former duties of the government-appointed Justice of the Peace. The 1894 Act created the 164 municipal boroughs, urban districts and rural districts. Each had a local administration responsible to a directly elected local council which replaced the appointed Boards responsible for the poor law and public health.

In all of this there was nothing distinctively 'Welsh'. The new structures were devised at Westminster with no distinction made between Wales and England. The domination of the previous structures of local administration by a Tory and Anglican gentry had been keenly resented by a Welsh population radicalised by the experiences of rapid industrialisation and a democratised dissenting religion. Thus the new structures were gratefully accepted but in no significant way initiated by Wales.

b) The politics of Welsh local government

In the 1889 elections to the new local authorities the Liberal Party gained 63 per cent of the seats and control of all but one of the 13 counties (Morgan, 1982). It remained in such a position of complete ascendancy for thirty years.

Welsh politics appears to tolerate only stability and consensus. In the 1920s it changed in perhaps the only possible way: suddenly and wholly to produce a new stability and a new consensus that remains even now, despite the occasional testing. Once the initial Liberal consensus broke up, rural and urban Wales quickly found and retained their own separate and different but pervasive conformity. Urban and industrial South Wales and North East Wales wholly adopted the Labour Party in the 1920s. Local government in these areas became subject to a Labour dominance rarely questioned and never successfully challenged. In 1990 in the urban districts and counties of Wales 67 per cent of councillors are Labour. Rural Wales emerged from the 1920s with an equal stability if less clarity. Formally independent councils emerged which largely maintain the values of the old Liberalism: mixing moderate measures of thrifty individualism, social democracy and a sometimes unpredictable localism. There is one consistency that links 1890 with 1990: in 1990 there were only two Conservative-controlled local authorities in Wales and the 20 Conservative county councillors in Wales made up less than 4 per cent of the total. The Tories have never been a party of local government in Wales.

The political stability of rural Wales is well portrayed by Balsom (1987) in his description of Ceredigion District:

> The 43 councillors are elected from 35 wards, many with small rural electorates of less than 500. It is thus easily possible for the local councillor to know well every family in his ward, especially so after so many years of being returned for the same district. In such circumstances, to be opposed at an election implies disrespect and if so challenged, the incumbent may well retire. (p 206)

In most of urban Wales the same stability has been provided by the Labour Party. Safe Labour wards provide councillors with the prospect of unchallenged occupancy of their position. Outside of Cardiff and Swansea, the Welsh Labour Party has had very little of the internal divisions found in parts of England. A traditional and still largely working-class Labour establishment dominates local government in urban Wales.

The stability of most of Welsh local government implies that there are not the periodic changes of electoral fortunes and therefore changes of council membership found in many parts of England. Therefore councillors tend to grow old in waiting for death to offer the release that may elsewhere be found in electoral defeat. Widdicombe (1986) found that 54 per cent of Welsh councillors are over 60, compared with 20 per cent in England. Ninety-five per cent of Welsh councillors are male compared with 80 per cent in England. Fifty per cent of Welsh councillors have a manual working background compared with 30 per cent in England.

Stability and consensus have clearly affected the style of local politics. One study of the policy process in Welsh local government provides the following description:

> In the Mid Glamorgan Labour Group there are no significant factions that one can identify as left and right, young or old. The relationships between the council leadership, other councillors and Labour Party members are ones of deference and patronage. With no acceptable means of challenge and succession, the leadership is elderly. ... Intra-party disputes in so far as they do emerge are based in the main on geographical, ward-based interests and committee loyalties. (Griffiths, 1987, p216)

II Structures and processes

a) The 1972 reforms

As in 1888 and 1894, Welsh local government was reformed by the 1972 Local Government Act on the same principles and by the same legislation as in England. This time, however, it might have been different. There was a decade of debate in Wales preceding the reform (Jones, 1986) and there were options for reform devised in Wales specifically for Wales. Ultimately a lack of agreement, perhaps a lack of interest, and probably a lack of nerve led the Welsh political establishment to accept an 'off-the-shelf' English package.

Designing a local government system for Wales is never going to be easy. There is a geographical divide that coexists with the political divide and which is equally stark. Of the Welsh population of 3 million, 60 per cent live in the 17 urban districts of South Wales which take up only 15 per cent of the land mass of Wales. The other 1.2 million Welsh people are thinly spread over 85 per cent of the land mass with an average population density of 0.63 people per hectare. This part of Wales has a lower population density than Northumberland, the most sparsely populated county in England.

The debate for the last local government reform in Wales began in earnest in 1958, when a Local Government Commission for Wales was established to consider the county and county borough boundaries. In 1963 it recommended the reduction in the number of counties from 13 to 7. Already the view that efficient local government was related to a larger scale of operation was becoming established. In 1965 an inter-departmental working party was established in the Welsh Office to examine the functions and boundaries of all classes of local authorities in Wales. Consulting with many advisers from within Welsh local authorities, this working party considered the range of options which continue to be debated within Welsh local government. It considered the establishment of single-tier authorities throughout Wales but baulked at the challenge of breaking up the prestigious and powerful Glamorgan County Council with its population of 750,000. Instead the working party recommended a two-tier structure of five counties, thirty-six districts and three county boroughs (Welsh Office, 1967).

This Welsh model was overtaken by events in England. In 1969 the Redcliffe Maud Commission recommended for England single-tier local authorities with optimum populations of over 500,000. Immediately, the Welsh Office lost faith in its own plans and tried to apply Redcliffe Maud to Wales. In 1970 a new White Paper (Welsh Office, 1970) proposed three unitary authorities for urban Wales with populations varying from 400,000 to 900,000. At the same time rural Wales would have a two-tier structure wherein the population of the upper tier would be as small as 116,000. In 1971 the new Conservative Government formally rejected the arguments of Redcliffe Maud and decided upon a two-tier structure that incorporated the former county boroughs into the new counties (Welsh Office, 1971). On this basis, the current system of local government was devised and consists of eight counties and thirty-seven districts.

In addition the 1972 Act gave much of Wales a third tier of over 700 community and town councils. In the three rural counties of Dyfed, Powys and Gwynedd there is comprehensive coverage by these local councils. In urban Wales coverage is more patchy - they hardly exist at all in the former boroughs of Cardiff, Swansea, Newport, Merthyr and Rhondda.

b) The Welsh Office

The Government of Wales and, indirectly, the local government of Wales has changed substantially as a result of the establishment of the Welsh Office in 1965. However, the original deployment of 200 civil servants with a Secretary of State in Cardiff was not thought by many to be more than a symbolic gesture. Initially the Welsh Office was perceived as a small co-ordinating unit for the executive work in Wales of the traditional, functional Whitehall departments. It has grown into a large department with over 2,000 civil servants in Cardiff, with a capacity to interpret, amend and, on occasion, initiate policy. It is now clearly responsible for the execution of government policy in Wales as it relates to local government, local government finance, education, economic and regional policy, health, housing, social services, industrial policy, agriculture, transport and planning.

These responsibilities alone would make the Welsh Office a dominant actor in Welsh politics and society. However, as the Welsh Office has grown, so many other parts of the state administrative system have had to develop Welsh structures in order to relate to it effectively (Osmond, 1985). There are now 42 public bodies structured to provide a service specifically to Wales and controlled by the Welsh Office (Cabinet Office, 1989). Economic and land-use planning in Wales is much influenced by the Welsh Development Agency, the Development Board for Rural Wales, the Land Authority for Wales, the Wales Tourist Board and the Countryside Council for Wales. The Welsh Sports Council and Play Wales co-ordinate and plan for the development of recreational facilities, and The Welsh Arts Council is the vehicle for the government sponsorships of the arts. Tai Cymru (Housing for Wales) is the Welsh equivalent of the English Housing Corporation, financing and co-ordinating the housing associations in Wales. All these organisations have been introduced in the wake of the establishment of the Welsh Office.

c) Policy communities in Wales

It is interesting to note how policy communities have been formed in Wales in response to the 'Welshification' of administrative and political structures. Consider, for example, the housing policy community which has been generated by the existence of a housing division at the Welsh Office. In response to the creation of Tai Cymru in 1989, the housing associations were encouraged to create Welsh structures and so, for instance, the United Kingdom Housing Trust which had been active in Wales was pressurised into forming the United Wales Housing Trust. Together the Welsh housing associations form the Welsh Federation of Housing Associations. The Institute of Housing in 1987 formed the Institute of Housing in Wales with an office in Cardiff. Pressure groups like Shelter and the Tenant Participation Advisory Service have formed distinct Welsh structures. The Welsh Office encouraged the formation of the Welsh Centre for Housing Management and Development at Cardiff University. The Welsh Office finances housing consultancy services such as Housing Options Wales, the Welsh Housing Management Advisory Panel and Priority Estates Projects Wales. This active and substantial policy community has just financed its own journal *Welsh Housing Quarterly*. This is just one example of a Welsh policy community: others include the media, education, health care and planning.

Such institutional development has had a profound effect on local government in Wales. In contrast to the position in 1965, it is now justified to refer to a Welsh system of local government.

d) Central-local relations in Wales

The relationship between central and local government is undertaken through entirely different channels in Wales and England. In Wales, the focus is almost entirely the Welsh Office, its Secretary of State, Minister of State and Parliamentary Under-Secretary of State. Welsh Office officials describe themselves as a "one-stop shop" for all who wish to participate in the administrative politics of Wales. The only Welsh local government services which maintain a direct relationship with Whitehall are the police service, the fire service and the probation service. In order to conduct this relationship the Welsh local authorities have created since 1974 their own associations: the Assembly of Welsh Counties and the Council of Welsh Districts. Whilst both organisations are formally part of the London-based

Association of County Councils and the Association of District Councils, they are accountable to their own member councils, and appear to have autonomy in developing the policy proposals they put to the Welsh Office.

The formal consultation between the Welsh Office and Welsh local authorities takes place through the Welsh Consultative Council for Local Government Finance and the Welsh Housing Consultative Council. Formal consultations between the local authorities and the Welsh quangos take place through forums such as the Liaison Committee between Tai Cymru and the Council of Welsh Districts, the Welsh Committee for Industrial and Economic Affairs and the Welsh Strategic Planning Advisory Committee. Less formally there is a network of personal relationships between the Welsh Office, the quangos and the local authorities. In addition, and significantly, as in the housing example, there is still a developing network of professional relationships represented in the different policy communities.

The financial role of the Welsh Office is central to the working of the whole system and illustrates its dual character, as an agent of the centre in the localities and a representative of the localities in the centre. A Welsh Office official explained that there is a:

> ... creative tension between the Welsh Office and the Treasury. The Welsh Office attempts to get the appropriate level for Wales ... once the resources are in then they become the financial controllers. They try to influence local authority spending.

Since 1981-2 the Welsh Office has had responsibility for negotiating the total amount of funding to be made available. As well as negotiating for the global amount, the Welsh Office allocates it between authorities using formulae which have been developed in Wales and are in form and principle different to those in England. The Welsh local authority associations are consulted on the allocation of resources to local authorities through the presence of their two associations on the Welsh Consultative Council on Local Government Finance. The ability of the Welsh Office to switch expenditure between policy areas can be significant. For example, the Welsh Office initiative on mental health and mental handicap has benefited from the investment of substantial new sums, in contrast to the initiative in England which is implemented within existing resources. By English standards, the size of the network of central-local relations is small. Personal relationships are easily forged and this leads to a distinctive informality (Goldsmith, 1987). Welsh Office staff feel that they know the responsible managers in Welsh local authorities and "can appreciate the restraints under which they work". The whole informal network of relationships is believed by many participants and observers to lead to more effective consultation and a more genuine partnership in the processes of executive decision and implementation (Madgwick and James, 1979). A Welsh Office official commented that:

> There is a general perception that Wales operates a system of 'good government' in the sense that strong relationships exist between local authorities and the Welsh Office which facilitate decision-making and increase a 'partnership' approach.

However, the closely knit networks of administrative and professional relationships can be interpreted in a very different way. What might be perceived as an open and consultative partnership at one time, may be perceived as top-down manipulation at another time. The network of informal relationships may be a channel for a genuine two-way flow of information. Alternatively, it may be used by the Welsh Office to communicate a selection of chosen messages, with persuasion, control of information and a range of incentives.

The balance of 'partnership' and 'control' is reflected in the following comment by a local housing manager who stated that relationships with the Welsh Office are:

> good on a personal level ... but the special relationship often consists of them still saying 'no' ... but in the nicest possible way.

III Outputs of the Welsh local government system

a) Welsh legislation and circulars

The administration of the Welsh Office is conducted within the parameters of Westminster legislation. Only rarely has the Welsh Office sought to amend that legislation. Still more rarely has it sought to initiate its own legislation. Welsh Office officials are keen to be perceived as part of the "Whitehall Village" - "This is a Whitehall department that happens to be located in Cardiff". It prefers that its influence on legislation should be within the Whitehall negotiations and the conventions of cabinet government that seek consensus and consistency across the United Kingdom. To break ranks and propose separate legislation might be seen as accepting isolation from the Whitehall village and leading to a reduction of status and influence.

Almost all the legislation that is unique to Wales refers to the Welsh language (either directly or indirectly) or to differences in the system of finance. There are some legislative differences in other areas. Thus under the 1972 Local Government Act waste disposal and the disposal of abandoned vehicles were designated District responsibilities rather than County as in England. There were also provisions made for libraries, certain agricultural functions and some Weights & Measures and Food & Drugs functions to be carried out by the Districts. As a result of regulations made under this Act, Cynon Valley DC, Merthyr Tydfil BC, Rhondda BC and Llanelli BC are all library authorities.

The acquisition of land for development is carried out by the Land Authority for Wales. Local authorities in England and the Land Authority in Wales were given responsibilities for the functions specified in the Community Land Act 1975. When this was repealed in 1980 the Land Authority for Wales was retained. Local authorities in Wales have the opportunity to contribute to the National Eisteddfod (National Eisteddfod Act 1959), the International Eisteddfod (Llangollen International Musical Eisteddfod Act 1967) and the Welsh National Opera (Welsh National Opera Act 1971). The Welsh Language Act 1967 enables the Secretary of State for Wales to order Welsh versions of statutory forms. Specific grants for the teaching of the Welsh language, or other subjects in that language are available from the

Secretary of State (Education Act 1980). Under the Education Reform Act 1988 the study of the Welsh language is one of the 'core' subjects and is mandatory for Welsh designated schools. In other schools it is a foundation subject.

An analysis of circulars issued by the Welsh Office between 1974 and 1989 similarly shows a minimum content of anything that might be described as 'uniquely Welsh'. In most cases the Welsh Office have added nothing more than a Welsh Office stamp and a Welsh language translation. The actual number of circulars issued by the Welsh Office ('English' and 'Welsh' policies) has declined from 282 in 1974 to 68 in 1989. This can be explained by the removal of many detailed controls over local authorities in the Local Government Planning and Land Act 1980. However, the percentage that dealt with 'Welsh' policies has increased from 5.3 per cent (average between 1974-79) to 9.3 per cent (average between 1980-89). This does not necessarily mean that the Welsh Office operates tighter control; 'Welsh' circulars are limited to a few policy areas so new legislation in one of those areas often explains the higher percentage. The number of circulars varies considerably across policy areas. The highest number that were 'specifically Welsh' dealt with Highways and Transport, Land and the Welsh Language.

b) Local government finance

Welsh local authorities spend more and are more generously funded by central government than comparable local authorities in England. Tables 1 and 2 in Appendix 1 present figures for the Welsh local government system and English non-metropolitan areas, which is the part of the English system that is most directly comparable with Wales. The figures show the combined position of counties and districts.

The total net current expenditure of Welsh authorities is around 20 per cent higher than that of English authorities. In almost all major service areas the level of expenditure in Wales is substantially greater. In many services the higher level of spending is associated with higher needs and higher costs of provision. For example, compared with English shires, Wales has more unemployment and poverty, and worse housing conditions (see *Regional Trends*). These characteristics lead to higher needs for education, the personal social services and economic development. The level of spending on police reflects a higher level of serious crime, and spending on fire services reflects a higher proportion of areas in 'high risk' categories (see *Local Government Comparative Statistics*). These higher needs are compounded by population sparsity which may lead to higher costs in services such as education, fire, highways and refuse collection (see Bennett, 1980).

The higher needs and costs of Welsh local authorities have produced higher central assessments of expenditure requirements. According to central government, the spending required to provide a 'standard' level of service is 16-22 per cent higher in Wales than in the English shires. The lower level of economic prosperity in Wales has also affected local government finance through the rateable values of domestic and business properties. Under the pre-1990 financial regime, the value of Welsh councils' tax base per capita was 27 per cent lower than in England. This difference has now formally disappeared: under the poll tax all authorities possess the same notional tax base per adult.

The higher needs and lower tax base of Welsh councils has contributed to higher levels of central grant support (See Table 2). Throughout the 1980s grant cuts were imposed in both England and Wales, but the decline in grant funding was much steeper in England. Thus the relative 'grant advantage' of Welsh councils has grown substantially since 1979: per capita grants are now more than twice as high as in England. This grant advantage is reflected in lower local tax bills: in 1990/1 the average poll tax was £232 in Wales and £360 in the English non-metropolitan areas.

Is the grant advantage of Welsh local authorities simply a result of their higher needs and lower tax base? Or do Welsh councils receive more favourable financial treatment from central government? In order to investigate this issue, a regression model was used to test the determinants of counties' block grant receipts in the 1980s (See Appendix 2).

The empirical results reflect the aim of block grant to compensate for need and resource differences (Boyne, 1989). Thus service needs have a positive effect on block grant and the local tax base has a negative effect. However, need and resource differences do not provide a complete explanation of grant variations. Even taking their higher needs and lower tax base into account, Welsh counties enjoy a significant grant advantage over English counties. If the evidence is interpreted in the context of mean grant levels, then, at any given level of needs and tax base, a Welsh county can expect to receive grant funding around 10 per cent higher than an English county. A 'technical' explanation of this grant advantage would be that it compensates for higher Welsh needs that are not fully reflected in the centre's assessment of expenditure requirements. A more political, and probably more plausible explanation, is that the additional funding reflects the success of the Welsh Office in securing money for Welsh local government. English non-metropolitan areas have no similar central ally to fight for funds on their behalf.

IV Conclusion

The Welsh local government system is different from the English system in three important respects. First, the formal **structure of the system** is distinctive. The structure of local government and the distribution of functions is largely the same as in England, but the structure of central government is very different. The Welsh Office combines functions spread across a variety of departments in England, and acts both on behalf of Whitehall in Wales and on behalf of Wales in Whitehall.

Second, the **processes** of central-local relations in Wales have been transformed by the establishment of the Welsh Office. The role of the Welsh Office has generated the growth of Welsh pressure groups and quangos, and resulted in a network of separate Welsh policy communities. The small number of Welsh local authorities has facilitated close and personal contacts between the Welsh Office and Local Authority staff.

Thirdly, the **outputs** of the Welsh system are different from the English system. There is little legislation that is uniquely Welsh, save for the major issue of the Welsh language. However, there is scope for Welsh Office discretion in the interpretation of national legislation, and room for policy innovations such as that on community care for the mentally handicapped. Central grants are higher in Wales, partly because of the high needs and low resources of Welsh councils. The higher level of grant funding in turn supports a higher level of expenditure in total and on all major areas of service provision.

In sum, these distinctive structures, processes and outputs are sufficient to substantiate the argument that there is a separate Welsh local government system. In subsequent chapters we consider the autonomy of local councils from central constraints, the emerging pattern of service delivery, and arguments for the establishment of a more distinct institutional framework for local government in Wales.

CHAPTER 3

CENTRAL POLICIES AND LOCAL AUTONOMY

THIS CHAPTER IS AN analysis of the autonomy of Welsh local authorities, with particular emphasis on the impact of central constraints since 1979. Part I of the chapter considers the meaning of 'local autonomy' and summarises the many forces that limit local policy decisions. Part II identifies two dimensions of local autonomy that central government may seek to influence: the autonomy of the local government system in the aggregate and, within the aggregate pattern, the autonomy of individual councils. Part III presents evidence on the impact of central policies on these two dimensions of local autonomy. Part IV identifies the services which display the highest and lowest degrees of diversity across local areas, and explores why some services are provided more uniformly than others. Part V draws conclusions on the relationship between central policies and local autonomy. The various tables can be found in Appendix 1.

I The concept of local autonomy

Local autonomy may be defined as the freedom to exercise choice in local policy-making. Autonomy implies local choice over the goals of local authority activities and the methods of achieving these goals (Clark, 1984). Thus local autonomy is reduced by central policies which remove powers of action or impose an obligation to act. Similarly, local autonomy is increased by policies which bestow powers or abolish obligations.

It should be noted that local authority autonomy is not valuable in itself (see Page, 1982; Bulpitt,1983). The main rationale for democratic local government is to match variations in public policies with variations in public preferences. However, local authorities may 'abuse' their autonomy and produce policies that fail to reflect local needs or demands. The freedom of local authorities to exercise choice in policy-making should not be equated with the freedom of local citizens to have the policies of their choice.

Some constraints on local autonomy are external to the local area: the European Community, central government, the national 'community' of local government and professional organisations. There are also constraints on local policy-making that are internal to the local area, but external to the authority itself: private companies, the local tax base, other parts of the public sector, pressure groups and the 'needs' of the public for service provision. The main focus of this research is on central-local relationships. Therefore, the primary aim is to evaluate the degree of central constraints on local choice.

II The forms and instruments of central constraints on local autonomy

Central constraints on local autonomy can take two forms. First, central government may shift the local government system as a whole (or a particular class of authorities) in a specific direction. For example, curbing council-house sales in the 1970s, or promoting council-house sales in the 1980s. This form of central constraint involves moving local government in the aggregate in a direction that it would not independently choose. Such policies represent a reduction of 'aggregate autonomy'; correspondingly, the removal of prescriptive or proscriptive policies would represent an increase in aggregate autonomy. All national governments in the UK have sought to impose this form of constraint on the local government system as a whole. Politicians in central government might claim that they have a mandate for such policies on the basis of their manifesto commitments and electoral success. The interesting issue that arises is whether central constraints on aggregate autonomy have been any greater since 1979 than in previous periods. There is no rigorous evidence on this issue, but the perceptions of many participants and observers imply that central constraints have increased greatly. For example, Loughlin (1986, p200) argues that "centralisation has been an inexorable process under the Conservative government". Similarly Travers (1989, p14) states that "the period from 1979-87 appears as one of unparalleled reduction in local autonomy".

A second form of central constraint is on the degree of local policy diversity within the level of aggregate autonomy. For example, given a central policy to cut spending in local government as a whole, to what extent is the level of spending across individual areas uniform or diverse? Constraints on 'individual autonomy' are also an established part of central-local relations: capital finance of individual councils has always been regulated (Ball, 1980), and revenue spending has always been manipulated through specific grants (Foster *et al*, 1980). However, it may be argued that the distinguishing characteristic of central constraints in the 1980s has been the interference in the policies of individual authorities and the attempt to impose uniformity on the local government system. For example, Butcher *et al* (1989, p5) argue that the direction of government policy since 1979 "has been towards the weakening of local choice and the containment of local variability in service provision". Similarly, Smith (1988, p235) argues that "since 1979, the U.K. government has embarked on an unprecedented programme to alter the behaviour of local authorities ... central to the government's campaign has been a desire to make the local authority sector more homogeneous".

The reduction of local autonomy is generally attributed to three instruments of central control: **law** (for example, rate-capping, competitive tendering, Right-to-Buy), **finance** (for example, capital allocation, grant penalties, specific grants) and the **monitoring of performance** (for example, inspectorates, the Audit Commission). However, our concern in this analysis is not to list the methods or extent of central constraints in principle. This has been well-covered elsewhere (for example, Cross and Bailey, 1986; Rhodes, 1988). Rather we seek to evaluate the autonomy of Welsh local government in practice.

Empirical analyses of the 'centralisation thesis' have sought to refute it by showing that there is local policy diversity (for example, Boaden, 1970; Danziger, 1978; Sharpe and Newton, 1984). However, such analyses focus on only one dimension of local autonomy: the autonomy of individual councils. A full assessment of central constraints must also examine the autonomy of local government in the aggregate. Therefore the analysis in the next section covers both forms of central constraints on local policy-making.

III The autonomy of Welsh local government
As Page (1980, p120) argues, "The manner in which central government seeks to influence the behaviour of local authorities cannot be adequately defined and measured without reference to some conception of the 'goals' of central government". The following analysis outlines central objectives with respect to 'aggregate' and 'individual' autonomy, and evaluates whether these objectives have been achieved.

a) Aggregate autonomy
Three broad objectives of the Conservative government in the 1980s can be identified: reductions in local government expenditure; a shift away from direct provision towards mixed or market provision; and a greater emphasis on market criteria in the provision of services.

i) Expenditure cuts?
Since 1979 the Conservative government has sought to reduce the overall scale of local authority activity and the level of spending funded from central and local taxation.

The figures in Table 3 (see Appendix 1) show that the desired effect on spending has not been achieved. Gross revenue spending had fallen slightly after the IMF cuts imposed by the Labour government in the 1970s; but since 1979 it has risen by around 20 per cent. Thus the 'turnover' of local government has continued to expand in real terms. Net revenue spending has also increased in recent years, after falling in the 1970s and mid-1980s. Over the whole period since 1979, revenue expenditure has grown by around 12 per cent. Finally, capital expenditure has also increased in real terms since 1979. During the 1970s the local authority capital programme was cut in half. In the 1980s the level of capital spending has fluctuated, but is now higher than in 1979.

ii) Less direct provision?

A lower level of direct provision should be reflected in lower staffing levels in local authorities. Table 4 shows that, from a peak in 1979, local authority employment fell by around 7,600 by 1987. The figure has since increased again, but remains around 6,000 lower than the figure inherited by the Conservatives.

The area of direct provision that the Conservatives have attacked most vigorously and consistently is council housing. Table 4 shows that the local authority housing stock in Wales has declined by 76,000 dwellings since 1979. This has been achieved through encouraging sales and preventing new building. After creeping slowly upwards in the face of resistance by the Labour government in the 1970s, sales peaked in 1982 and surged upwards again in the late 1980s. By contrast, new building by local authorities has fallen throughout the 1980s. Between 1981 and 1989 local councils' share of all new building dwindled to 5 per cent.

Thus it may be concluded that the level of direct provision in general has been reduced, and that the direct provision of housing in particular has been cut substantially. Nevertheless, it is worth noting that a large council housing stock remains.

iii) Greater reliance on market criteria?

The emphasis on market criteria in local government is clearly expressed in the 'community charge', which is intended to be a flat-rate payment in exchange for a standard package of services. A greater reliance on market criteria of resource distribution also implies more income from fees and charges for specific services, lower subsidies for trading services, and less redistribution from local taxpayers to council tenants.

Table 5 shows that central policies have been successful on all three of these criteria. Income from fees and charges has risen since 1979, although not significantly more rapidly than in the 1970s. Similarly, rate fund subsidies to trading services have fallen under the Conservatives, but this also confirms a trend established under the Labour government. The most pronounced decline has been in the real level of redistribution from rate-payers to council tenants. This subsidy has dipped sharply since 1979, and from

April 1990 has been abolished completely.

Overall, then, the role of market criteria in local government has increased substantially. However, with the exception of housing subsidies, the Conservatives have simply accelerated existing trends rather than caused a sharp change in direction.

b) Autonomy of individual councils

This dimension of local government autonomy can be measured in three ways. First, by the extent to which councils conform with centrally specified targets. Second, by the degree of policy diversity. Third, by the strength of the relationship between local party control and local policy outputs. If the autonomy of individual councils has declined since 1979, then there should be evidence of greater compliance with central targets, more uniformity in policy decisions, and a weaker link between parties and policies. These issues are analysed below.

i) Greater compliance with central targets?

In general, Welsh local authorities conformed fairly closely with central judgements of expenditure need between 1981 and 1989. During this period the counties and districts did not stray more than 5 per cent and 8 per cent above their respective guidelines; and in two years district spending was *less* than specified by central government. In addition, Welsh authorities' spending as a percentage of GREA became more uniform over time (see coefficients of variation in Table 6). Thus between 1981 and 1989 councils' spending converged on a common position that gradually moved closer to central preferences.

This trend is highlighted by the figures for the councils with the highest spending in relation to their GREA. In the counties the average maximum 'overspend' was 12 per cent between 1981 and 1983, 9 per cent between 1984 and 1986, and 7 per cent between 1987 and 1989. The district figures for the same three periods were 42 per cent, 24 per cent and 17 per cent respectively.

The introduction of the new system of needs assessment and local government finance in 1990 has had little impact on the general pattern of compliance in the counties. By contrast, the new regime has thoroughly destabilised the position in the districts (See Table 6). It remains to be seen whether this is a new pattern of 'non-compliance'.

ii) Less policy diversity?

It has been argued that central government has pressed local authorities to adopt more uniform policies through instruments such as the publication of performance data and 'inspections' by the Audit Commission (Smith, 1988; Boyne and Law, 1991). If local authorities have succumbed to such pressures then policy diversity should have declined since 1979. (Tables 7 to 10 show coefficients of variation for a range of County and District policies. Figures for 1979/80 (or earlier) are used as a base point for comparison with two later periods in order to track changes in local policy diversity.)

The pattern for a wide range of county policies is shown in Table 7. There has been a definite decline in the diversity of net revenue spending per capita, which is probably attributable to increased compliance with central spending guidelines. However, few other policy outputs show such a clear trend towards uniformity. The only substantial and consistent fall in diversity is in the area of library policies. Otherwise the pattern is much the same as in 1979. There is little sign that local education outputs have become more uniform. If anything, diversity has increased, particularly in nursery provision and further education (see Table 8).

Figures for general indicators of district council policies are shown in Table 9. As in the case of the counties, most of the changes are small and resemble random fluctuations rather than a systematic decline. The only marked reductions in diversity are in refuse collection staffing, and revenue/cost ratios in recreation and trade and industrial estates. There are other small declines (for example, in rate collection) but these are counterbalanced by small increases in some areas (for example, museums, galleries and theatres). The level of council-house sales as a percentage of the council stock has become more uniform since the 1970s, but all five of the other housing policies display greater diversity over time (see Table 10).

iii) A weaker link between political parties and policy outputs?

In principle, local representative democracy allows the public to influence policies indirectly by swapping one set of politicians for another set. Thus, if local authorities possess political autonomy then the party colour of the council should be reflected in policy choices. However, it has been argued that since 1979 the Conservative government has sought to restrain local party effects and, in particular, to fetter the policies of Labour councils (Duncan and Godwin, 1988; Stoker, 1988). This was expressed most crudely by Margaret Thatcher's desire to "eradicate socialism" from British politics.

In order to establish whether party effects have become weaker since the 1970s, it is first necessary to specify the types of policies that parties are expected to influence. On the basis of their proclaimed ideological preferences, it may be hypothesised that Labour councils will provide a higher level of local services in general and will show a stronger commitment to redistributive services that benefit lower income groups (Sharpe and Newton, 1984).

The extent of a council's commitment to service provision can be indicated by the level of spending in relation to the spending required to provide a 'standard' level of services. The evidence in Table 11 shows that both counties and districts under Labour control score above average on this indicator. The pattern in the counties has been stable since 1981. The link between party control and district spending became stronger in the mid-1980s, but then declined.

Table 11 also provides evidence on the association between Labour control and redistributive policies. Few public services are substantially redistributive in practice (Goodin and Le Grand, 1987). Nevertheless, there is evidence of a bias in favour of lower income groups in the distribution of the personal social services (Bramley *et al*, 1989) and council housing (Le Grand, 1982). These two services were therefore selected to test the relationship between political parties and redistribution in the counties and districts respectively.

All the significant associations between Labour control and the personal social services are in the expected positive direction.

Over time the link between party control and service provision has generally become stronger. The pattern for housing policies is more mixed. The relationship between Labour control and new building has become weaker since the 1970s, possibly because of central restrictions on capital spending. The link between Labour control and council-house sales has also become less significant. This may reflect a greater central grip on local decisions, or a weakening of local Labour resistance in the wake of the party leadership's change of heart on this issue. The evidence shows no significant link between rent levels and Labour control. By contrast, rate fund subsidies became more strongly associated with Labour control in the 1980s, but this relationship tapered off in the period prior to the abolition of this subsidy in 1990.

On balance, then, there has been little change in local political autonomy since 1979. The impact of party control has become weaker in some policy areas, but stronger in others.

c) **Summary**
The main effect of central constraints in the 1980s has been on aggregate autonomy rather than individual autonomy. The local government system as a whole has been moved in the direction of less direct provision and more reliance on market criteria of resource allocation. By contrast, within the aggregate pattern, individual councils retain the autonomy to adopt distinctive policies; and Labour councils continue to spend above average and provide higher levels of redistributive services.

IV Variations in diversity across services
This section assesses the relative diversity of policy outputs in different service areas, and examines why some services are geographically uniform while other services are geographically diverse (see Table 12). In order to provide an external reference point, the figures for Welsh councils in the 1980s are compared with county boroughs and county councils in the pre-1974 local government system. Differences in policy diversity across services may to some extent reflect differences in the diversity of service needs. However, it should be noted that many of the policy indicators are measured on a 'per client' basis; for example,

education provision per pupil or social service provision per elderly person. In addition the whole population is the 'client group' for some services and therefore the per capita measures provide a rough control for variations in needs. These characteristics of the policy indicators serve to reduce the potentially distorting effects of different variations in service needs.

There are striking similarities in the relative diversity of service outputs in the Welsh authorities and in the pre-1974 county boroughs and county councils. Education is the least diverse service and the secondary pupil/teacher ratio is the most uniform policy indicator regardless of the time period or the group of authorities that are examined. The police service and total spending are the other areas which display the least diversity. Policy indicators for the personal social services, the fire service and libraries generally occupy a middle position in Table 12. The service areas which show most diversity are housing, highways, planning, recreation and cultural facilities.

This stability in the pattern of policy diversity has two implications for an attempt to explain why some services are more uniform than others. First, the major sources of relative diversity are unlikely to be specific to Wales, but rather are likely to be characteristics of the English and Welsh local government system as a whole. Second, the extent of diversity in different services is not simply the product of contemporary local choices or constraints. Rather, the broad pattern has been fixed for some time, and must therefore be explained historically.

Three broad characteristics appear to differentiate diverse services from uniform services:

• **The statutory basis of service provision**
As Loughlin (1986, 2) notes, "local government law is primarily concerned with powers rather than duties". Nevertheless, the balance of powers and duties varies across services and this may explain why some services are more diverse than others. For example, local authorities are empowered but not obligated to provide recreational facilities and museums, galleries and theatres. These service areas display high diversity. By contrast, councils

have a duty to provide the police service, and a duty to ensure the provision of a sufficient quantity and quality of schools. These service areas display low diversity. However, a statutory obligation to provide a service is not in itself a sufficient condition for uniform provision. For example, local authorities have a duty to provide a comprehensive and efficient library service (Cross and Bailey, 1986), but the outputs of this service are not amongst the most uniform.

• **The role of central government inspectorates**
The main services in which inspectorates operate are education, police and fire (see Cross and Bailey, 1986). The inspectorates for schools and constabulary were established in the mid-nineteenth century and are the most long-standing (Rhodes, 1981). The presence of central inspectorates throughout the development of these services probably contributes to the high uniformity of the policy indicators.

• **The level of professionalisation of service provision**
Common professional standards of service provision may produce uniformity across local authorities. The most highly professionalised services include education and the police. The personal social services are staffed by a mixture of professionals and non-professionals, and display a moderate degree of diversity. In housing the main professions are characterised by "weakness and low status" (Houlihan, 1988, p203), and this service area shows a high level of diversity.

Thus central constraints of legislation and inspection may partly explain why some services are provided on a more uniform basis than others, but it is likely that professional standards also contribute to uniformity. When all three of these forces occur together, as in the case of education, the result is a low degree of diversity. When all three of these forces are absent, as in the case of recreational and cultural facilities, the result is a high degree of diversity.

V Conclusion

Four main conclusions can be drawn from the analysis in this chapter. First, there has been some decline in the aggregate autonomy of Welsh local government in the 1980s. Central government has sought expenditure cuts, less direct provision and more reliance on market criteria of resource distribution. The first of these objectives has not been achieved, but the latter two have been. Thus the local government system as a whole has moved in some of the directions that central government desired. This can be interpreted as a decline in aggregate autonomy, assuming that local authorities would not independently have chosen these policies. Such losses of local autonomy are, to some extent, counterbalanced by gains in autonomy that are frequently overlooked. For example, the 1979 Education Act removed the obligation on local authorities to submit plans for the 'comprehensive' reorganisation of secondary education. Similarly, the 1980 Housing Act bestowed the power on local authorities to make a profit on their Housing Revenue Account.

Second, there has been little change in the autonomy of individual councils within the aggregate pattern. The Conservative governments have sought compliance with central guidelines, less policy diversity and less political autonomy on the part of Labour councils. Only the first of these three aims has been achieved: Welsh councils have conformed closely with central spending guidelines. The degree of diversity in most policy areas has altered little since the 1970s, and the link between party control and policy outputs remains largely intact. It may be argued that central-local relations in the 1980s were like a game of 'cat and mouse'. However, a better analogy is a game of cat and *mice*: dozens of them, running behind the back, between the legs and beyond the reach of the centre.

Third, central constraints appear to be an important long-term influence on the degree of diversity in different policy areas. There is more geographical uniformity in service provision when legislation imposes duties rather than powers, and when central departments deploy inspectorates to regulate minimum standards and foster efficiency. However, 'noncentral' influences such as professionalism also partly explain why some services are more uniform than others. Finally, there is little sign of a 'crisis' of local autonomy in the 1980s. It is important not to overemphasise the impact of central attempts to constrain local autonomy. Some analyses claim that local autonomy has been 'destroyed' (Duncan and Godwin, 1988; see also Newton and Karran, 1985). Such claims seem to overlook the lessons from studies of policy implementation: there is likely to be a substantial gap between central objectives and local behaviour. For example, cuts in grant have influenced, but by no means 'controlled', local spending decisions (Boyne, 1990). The evidence presented in this chapter indicates that Margaret Thatcher did not, after all, single-handedly bridge the implementation gap. And in Wales, at least, reports of the death of local autonomy are an exaggeration.

CHAPTER 4

THE ROLE OF LOCAL AUTHORITIES: ENABLERS OR PROVIDERS?

T HE AIM OF THIS chapter is to examine variations in the style of local service provision in Wales, both in the counties and the districts. We characterise these variations according to general principles concerning different models of local authority roles. We provide a general overview of such variations and then concentrate upon the provision of education, a county function, and housing, a district function. Information on these issues has been primarily derived from questionnaires that were sent to, and interviews that were conducted with, Chief Executives, Chief Education Officers and Chief Housing Officers (or their representatives). The combined response rates to the questionnaires and to our requests for interviews were as follows :

	Percentages
Chief Executives (counties)	65
Chief Executives (districts)	54
Chief Education Officers	50
Chief Housing Officers	84

The samples cover urban and rural areas, authorities in North, South, Mid and West Wales, and councils of various party political complexions. We have supplemented this material with information drawn from the academic literature and from relevant legislation and government documents.

Part I examines the theoretical framework and different role models of local government.(We provide a summary of the different styles of service delivery in Appendix 2.) Parts II, III and IV analyse the responses of officers in local government to our questionnaires and interviews. Part V summarises our findings.

I The theoretical framework

We can hypothesise that individual local authorities may be found on a continuum ranging from a minimalist role, where an authority meets once a year to hand out contracts to the private sector, to one of direct provision across a wide range of services.

In Chapter 3 we concluded that the level of direct service provision by local authorities has been cut, particularly in the field of housing. Similarly, we concluded that the role of market criteria in local government has increased substantially. However, we are still a long way from the minimalist local authority and we found little evidence of, or commitment to, this type of role. At the same time we have found evidence that many local authorities are concerned at the limitations being placed upon them in direct service provision.

It is appropriate to use, therefore, the following descriptions of local authority roles :

1. Enabler (market-driven)
2. Traditional (direct provider)
3. Enabler (participatory)

Clarke and Stewart (1989) distinguish between the traditional authority and the enabling authority. The assumptions of the traditional authority are that it is self-sufficient, production-orientated, perceives itself as the monopoly or majority producer of services, and seeks uniformity and the standardisation of its services.

Clarke and Stewart also distinguish between two types of enabling authority. They characterise one type as that which passes on the provision of services to others, allowing these other bodies to act on its behalf. We take the enabler (market-driven) role of our theoretical framework to conform to this definition of the enabling authority. In contrast to this Clarke and Stewart define a wider view of the enabling authority such that this type of authority will:

> use all means at its disposal to meet the needs of those who live within its area. It will produce some services itself. It will work with and through other organisations

- in the public, private and voluntary sectors - aiding, stimulating and guiding their contributions. (Clarke and Stewart, 1988, p1)

This definition of the enabling authority conforms to the enabling (participatory) authority of our theoretical framework. It is also the definition of the enabling authority that was endorsed by respondents to our questionnaire. A typical definition of the enabling authority given to us was:

The body for articulating the views of the community, whatever they might be, and then using its powers and influence to try and achieve them.

This role, however, was perceived to be nothing new. Indeed many of our respondents were keen to stress that they had been acting in an enabling manner for many years even though such activities may not have been articulated as 'enabling'.

At the same time it also became clear that, in many cases, the reliance upon others has been driven by limited resources rather than by the conscious decision to embrace a clearly articulated pluralist philosophy of participatory or community government. Such a philosophy would include the commitment to share powers and responsibilities with the organisations and associations of the wider community.

In practice we also found many examples of authorities conforming to the traditional role and the enabler (market-driven) role, even though our respondents may have been reluctant to admit that these roles characterised their authority.

It is also worth making the general point that *within* the same authority the enabling role (of either definition) may be supported for one activity but not for another. The clearest example of this is the different attitudes towards economic development and housing. Authorities are extremely willing to be innovative and to seek to foster partnerships with other bodies, public or private, in the field of economic development. In contrast to this, the same authority may resent its loss of responsibility for house-building and believe that it should be the main provider of social housing rather than, for example, a housing association. Such a contrast may not, of course, be irrational. Different services may require different models of provision. Nevertheless, there may be a clash of values within any one organisation.

Finally, both the definitions of the enabling role assume that there are other bodies, either in the private or voluntary sector, that exist to be 'enabled'. In Wales this is not always the case; for example, under compulsory competitive tendering almost all the services that went out to tender were won by the in-house tender. Notwithstanding the quality of the in-house bid, in many areas within Wales there was not, in fact, any competition. This may be the result of the small, sparsely populated rural character of many Welsh local districts. Such communities may not have the economic capacity to generate competing providers for local services and the value of the contract may be too small to attract tenders from outside the area.

II The Chief Executives' response

Information was gathered from Chief Executives of counties and districts. It was examined against a number of criteria which are mapped in Appendix 2.

a) Role emphasis

In general, many Welsh authorities may be characterised as traditional, believing that the authority should be providing services as its main role. One Chief Executive expressed the view that :

> The concept that local authorities should progressively cease to provide services directly and should increasingly contract services out to the private sector is an anathema to a council such as (X) which has a proud record of serving the community as a direct provider of varied and diverse services.

The unwillingness to embrace the enabling (market-driven) model, however, does not preclude the adoption of the enabling (participatory) role. Indeed we found many examples of authorities utilising other bodies to provide services. Some rural authorities have a long tradition of using the private sector to provide a wide range of specialist services. In addition, because of financial constraints more and more authorities are looking to other bodies, private and voluntary, to provide some services. The emphasis is on a *pragmatic* response to perceived constraints.

b) Role culture

The culture of many authorities can be characterised as reactive in the sense that many authorities respond to changing legislation rather than being pro-active and innovative. However, there are notable exceptions:

- a number of authorities have commissioned surveys by consultants to examine the future role of their authority.
- a number of authorities now have mission statements concerning their future roles. One county council, with the support of its district authorities, is preparing an 'image' profile to market itself both inside and outside the county.
- one Chief Executive described his role as "changing the culture of the authority" and is planning attitude surveys of employees to examine changes in values.
- *all* authorities surveyed indicated a change in culture brought about by legislation concerning compulsory competitive tendering. The process has led to much more commercial awareness and an increasing awareness of costs.

c) Strategic planning

As indicated above, a number of authorities are developing 'mission statements' to take their authorities into the mid-1990s. More common, however, is a strategic plan for one service area but not for other areas within the same authority. In the field of economic development, for example, authorities had clear ideas about the direction in which they were heading. Within the same authority other service areas were often characterised by departmentalism, by looking inwards rather than outwards. One authority with a clear economic development strategy was also described to us as a " ... nuts-and-bolts authority that delights in operational detail".

Concern was also expressed about the difficulty of developing a strategic plan for the authority as a whole where no one party has overall control or where the authority is dominated by independent members.

d) Basis of service provision

Most authorities use a combination of voluntary and private sector organisations to provide certain services where the local authority is not bound by statute to provide the service itself. In the smaller, rural areas, there is a long tradition of close co-operation with the voluntary sector. As one Chief Executive put it:

> I consider this (the use of voluntary bodies) to be a sensible use of limited resources as voluntary bodies generally have lower overheads.

It is also the case that in the rural areas any moves towards the market model of provision would be curtailed by the lack of private sector organisations to undertake the work.

e) Basis of internal organisation

To some extent internal organisation is a function of geography with many rural authorities relying upon area offices. This has been a feature of local government in Wales since 1974. In this sense, local authorities have been 'close to the customer' in providing local offices for advice, services and information. Such offices are generally seen as the administrative arm of the centre. In one urban district authority there is a move towards decentralisation as a conscious matter of policy and to set up 'one-stop shops' on a local basis.

Otherwise, we find examples of decentralisation in certain service areas such as housing or social services. In some authorities the centre plays a supervisory and co-ordinating role with day-to-day management left to the decentralised personnel. We also found a move towards the rationalisation of certain services at the centre. Competitive tendering arrangements or a cohesive marketing strategy are more easily accommodated at the centre.

Generally, the motive for organisational change tends to be pragmatic rather than because of any strong, ideological commitment to one form of internal organisation.

f) Political management structures

Even with decentralised offices the tendency in most authorities is for decisions to be taken at the centre over policy and finances. Several authorities are moving down the road of delegating responsibility for budgeting to officers at the 'coal face'. The exception is in the field of compulsory competitive tendering where management boards have been created. Such boards are often headed by a managing director with substantial autonomy. In one authority: "The service is run by a managing director who has complete autonomy and administers the services at arm's length."

It is in the area of competitive tendering arrangements that many local authorities come closest to the concept of the enabler (market-driven) role for local authorities.

g) Accountability

We examine this from three perspectives:

i) Political accountability

For the most part, the elected member is seen as the embodiment of political accountability. There is little evidence of direct accountability to the citizen through neighbourhood forums or area committees. There is some use of consumer surveys to elicit the views of those affected by a particular service. One view expressed was that:"Consumer surveys may be seen to undermine the role of the councillor".

ii) Financial accountability

There is an increasing awareness of financial accountability brought about by competitive tendering legislation. Cost centres are being identified and management information systems being developed. Although the increased awareness of financial accountability is welcomed the impact of compulsory competitive tendering has not always been without problems. In one authority: "Certain areas are suffering from shock. Occasionally they re-group for a counter-attack. Progress is not being made without pain".

iii) *Professional accountability*

Professional accountability through the use of, for example, performance indicators is very much in the formative stages. Some authorities suffer from a lack of management information systems and some officers respond more readily than others to such requirements. When asked to comment on what would make local government work better one officer suggested: "A push from within each authority to improve management processes and performance review systems". This is a view that is steadily gaining ground.

h) Discretion

Most local authorities are involved in economic development to a greater or lesser extent. Similarly, many authorities are involved in the provision of recreation and leisure facilities where legislation places no clear duty for provision. The environment is increasingly being placed on the agenda and in the case of Cardiff City Council forms a substantial part of its mission statement.

However, the overall perception seems to be one of reduced discretion through increased central government control particularly in the fields of education and housing. There is a feeling that the role of the local authority will be one of influence and monitoring rather than the control of service provision. According to one Chief Officer, the reforms of the 1980s: "... imply considerable reduction in 'traditional' services provided by local authorities. Direct service provision and scope for local choice have been curtailed."

In the areas of competitive tendering, many authorities would not have considered expanding the use of private sector organisations to provide services without the legislation.

However, such feelings concerning the loss of autonomy may not be borne out by an examination of the diversity across different policy areas and local political autonomy (see Chapter 3).

Indeed, many local authorities continue to be pro-active in areas such as economic development, the environment, leisure and recreation, and continue to work in innovative ways with other local authorities, private and voluntary sector organisations and with community groups.

i) Basis of relations with other authorities

With one or two exceptions the relations between the districts and the counties appear to be very good and we came across many examples of joint collaboration, provision and funding of services. Examples include: joint provision of sports and leisure facilities; joint support of tourism through such bodies as the Heart of Wales Tourist Association; joint economic surveys; joint liaison committees in social services and education.

In the rural areas in particular, officers in the districts indicated support for the community councils and welcomed the role that this tier of authority play as a forum for local opinion.

j) Basis of relations with other bodies (private and voluntary)

As indicated earlier, all local authorities, and in particular the rural ones, have strong links with the voluntary sector and these links are a way of life for these authorities. Such links cover rural recreation schemes, pre-school education, assistance to the arts and with bodies such as the Citizens Advice Bureaux.

Similarly, there are strong links with the private sector in areas such as economic development, urban regeneration and leisure and recreation. These links are brought together more formally in organisations such as the Heart of Wales Tourist Association and the Crown of Wales Association which promotes industry. The dominant force behind such links is often a pragmatic one: whatever is best for the local community irrespective of party politics or ideology.

Both (i) and (j) illustrate the existence of networking throughout much of local government in Wales. Strong links, often informal and personal have developed between different authorities, agencies and organisations and involving the Welsh Office.

k) Summary

Local government in Wales is pragmatic in nature. For the most part it may appear to be traditional but local authorities adopt either of the enabling roles, particularly the participatory version, where it is expedient to do so. Only in one or two authorities did we find evidence of a systematic commitment to the enabling (participatory) model being developed. Because of this pragmatic response there are different forms of service delivery within the same authority.

Any changes in the content and methods of service delivery have, for the most part, been driven by legislation in the form of compulsory competitive tendering; by the perceived lack of resources; and by the rural nature of many authorities within Wales.

III The response from education

The last decade has seen profound changes in the provision of education throughout England and Wales culminating in the Education Reform Act, 1988 (ERA). The changes brought about by this act included the introduction of the National Curriculum, the Local Management of Schools (LMS) and colleges (LMC), and extended financial delegation to schools.

The changes that have taken place reflect a number of different concerns. Growing fears over the quality of education and disparities in standards were increasingly voiced. At the same time, the adoption of market principles and consumer choice for education has been advocated in much the same way as in other areas of local government provision.

a) The Education Reform Act 1988

The Act provides for a National Curriculum comprising core and other foundation subjects and in Wales the Welsh language is treated as a core and a foundation subject depending upon the designation of the school. The Secretary of State can set attainment targets, programmes of study and assessment arrangements. The Secretary of State will be advised by, in Wales, the Curriculum Council for Wales appointed by the Secretary of State to review the curriculum for schools, advise and publish information. In the words of one commentator: "No LEA has ever directed the curriculum as the Secretary of State now can." (Leonard, 1988, p 40)

The Act also provides for the delegation of finance and management to secondary schools and primary schools having 200 or more registered pupils. In brief, the financial arrangements are as follows:

• The General Schools Budget is the amount appropriated to meet all expenditure on an LEA's schools for the financial year.

• The LEA then subtracts the amount it needs for the things it will continue to do. This amount is split into three parts; mandatory exceptions; discretionary exceptions (subject to 10 per cent limit); discretionary exceptions (not subject to 10 per cent limit)

• The remaining sum is the Aggregated Schools Budget which is shared among schools. At least 75 per cent of this sum has to be allocated on the basis of the number and ages of the schools' pupils.

The LEAs cannot delegate responsibility for capital expenditure or for government or EEC grants for specific projects. These are the mandatory exceptions.

Discretionary items approved by the particular LEA and subject to the 10 per cent limit include structural repairs and maintenance, education psychology and welfare services, LEA initiatives, peripatetic services and special staff costs (see Thomas, 1990).

Discretionary items approved by the particular LEA and not subject to the 10 per cent limit include school meals, home-to-school transport, premature retirement and dismissal of staff and central administration, including inspectors and advisers.

The new role of the LEA will include deciding the total amount to be spent on schools, providing central support services and monitoring the performance of schools.

b) The Welsh context

The role of the Welsh language has been at the heart of the debate over education in Wales. According to Madgwick and Rawkins (1982) conflict over the status of the Welsh language in schools has occurred throughout Wales. Section 21 of the 1980 Education Act allows for specific grants to be made to LEAs and other bodies for education in and through the Welsh language. However, despite the prominence of the language issue, the teaching of Welsh has been problematic. For example, the HMI report 'Some Aspects of Educational Provision in Wales' (1986/87) found that, despite improvement, standards in Welsh as a second language in primary schools remained, in some areas, disappointing. Similarly the National Audit Office report (1989) was critical of the role of the Welsh Office in monitoring the economy, efficiency and effectiveness of its Welsh language grants to local authorities and other bodies. Similarly, several Welsh LEAs have expressed concern over the lack of Welsh language teachers to meet the requirements of the National Curriculum.

In Chapter 3 we argued that local education outputs in Wales have become more uniform, with the possible exceptions of nursery school provision and in further education, and that education is the service which displays least policy diversity. Possible explanations include the importance of professionalism, the fact that it is for the most part bound by statutory obligations and the role of the inspectorate. A further factor may be the existence of the networking in Wales expressed in the role of the Welsh Office and the Welsh Joint Education Committee (which acts as an examination board and as a general forum for debate on issues affecting LEAs).

c) Features of education in Wales

We examine a number of features of styles of delivery in education.

(i) Role emphasis - refers to the values, culture and how LEAs perceive their role

(ii) Strategic management - refers to the role of the LEA in planning

(iii) Discretion - refers to the use of discretion given to LEAs by the Education Reform Act

(iv) Relations with other LEAs - refers to the extent to which LEAs engage in joint provision

(v) Service delivery - refers to the ways in which LEAs may seek to explore new methods of service delivery

We provide a map of these criteria against different models of local government in Appendix 2.

i) Role emphasis

Despite the limitations imposed by the ERA, several of our authorities had clear statements and commitments to the concept of community education and this commitment was long-standing. One authority's Education Management Plan expressed this role as:

> ... to act as a facilitator to prompt individuals, institutions, establishments and organisations within a community to become aware of community development and the community needs of all members of the community.

All local authorities have been involved in curriculum development and have had long-standing language policies. Often this curriculum development has gone unrecognised. Several authorities indicated that they were moving towards an enabling role anyway and LMS has provided impetus. As one Chief Education Officer expressed it:

> LEAs have increasingly taken their democratic function to mean accountability over wider ranges of interest groups than ever before, including county councillors, parents, pupils and staff. The LEA is uniquely placed to provide a forum for discussion and debate as well as accountability to all these groups.

ii) Strategic Management

A number of authorities expressed concern that planning joint provision with other authorities and between different schools becomes more difficult under LMS. As one Chief Education Officer put it, strategic management is important:

> ... for agreeing shared values and establishing a meaningful partnership in order that it may be possible for us to plan joint provision - provision that would not be possible if institutions worked independently."

One authority indicated that it had had a strategic management plan prior to the ERA. Similarly, LEAs had developed strategic plans for the development of tertiary education.

iii) Discretion

There are a number of possibilities for discretion arising from the ERA, particularly in areas of financial delegation. Table 13 (Appendix 1) shows the variations in financial delegation between LEAs in Wales.

The discretionary (no limit) expenditure shows the greatest differences between the authorities. Items under this heading include school meals, home-to-school transport, central administration and inspectors and advisers. In rural areas we might find, therefore, higher expenditure on home-to-school transport which might account for relatively higher expenditure in Powys and Gwynedd compared to South and West Glamorgan. High central administration costs might be explained by high expenditure on advisers and inspectors. Variations in the discretionary (10 per cent limit) expenditure could be explained by the state of the school buildings and their repair and maintenance.

Other areas of discretion include the expenditure on the non-statutory areas of education provision such as pre-school education, youth organisations and adult education. Our survey indicated variations in expenditure on voluntary education provision such as nursery education ranging from 0.6 per cent to 0.2 per cent of the education budget. Variations in expenditure on adult education were more extreme and ranged from 0.21 per cent of the education budget to 1.6 per cent of the education budget.

Given that these areas are open to discretion we would expect variations here to reflect a change in perceptions of the role of authorities. For example, the enabling (participatory) authority is likely to make a larger contribution to voluntary agencies than either of the other two types of authority. Several authorities indicated extensive collaboration with voluntary bodies such as playgroup associations, youth work organisations,and family support groups. Similarly, several authorities saw the provision of adult education as part of a wider commitment to community education and one authority has created District Adult Training Education Committees based upon the catchment area of its tertiary colleges.

iv) *Relations with other authorities*

In most authorities there appears to be much evidence of joint activities. Gwynedd and West Glamorgan are part of a group of LEAs developing the use of satellite broadcasting as a teaching and learning aid. Gwynedd, Powys and Clwyd provide a North Wales database of information on training opportunities. Several authorities expressed concern that under LMS such joint activities may be more difficult to engage in.

The Welsh Joint Education Committee acts as a forum for education authorities to discuss examination matters, language and curriculum development. There are also formal and informal links with the Welsh Office although, according to one Chief Education Officer: "Pressure of change gives little room for proper consultation and constructive dialogue."

The Welsh Office perceive their relations with LEAs to be good and indicate co-operation in submitting LMS schemes on time. At the same time, the Welsh Office have indicated that they are looking for a reduction in the proportion of expenditure retained by the LEA.

v) *Service Delivery*

Given the rural nature of much of Wales, LEAs have looked to pursue innovative methods of service delivery through the use of distance learning. This role may become more important following the ERA. As one Chief Education Officer expressed it:

> With the content of the curriculum largely determined, the main thrust of the authority's influence will be in the direction of strengthening teaching methods and encouraging alternative modes of delivery.

The ERA has meant a change in the role of the LEA; one of our respondents indicated that:

> The decrease in power over a number of issues, particularly since the 1988 Act, but, arguably, pre-dating that, has meant an increase in the support, advice and guidance functions. This has led to a change in working styles as well as in content.

Several authorities have responded to this change in working styles with officers and advisers working together in providing the monitoring role. In two authorities this is being done through area teams.

d) Summary

There appears to be much evidence of Welsh LEAs moving in similar directions and having close contacts with each other. We find many examples of Welsh LEAs being innovative and pro-active in seeking out new forms of service delivery and in areas of joint provision. Welsh LEAs see their roles positively following on from the Education Reform Act and see themselves as part of a network, involved in partnerships with the service providers. Welsh LEAs tend to retain a large proportion of the General Schools Budget and are keen to play an important role in acting as a focus for educational provision in their authority.

Generally, then, Welsh LEAs can be located between the traditional and the enabling (participatory) models of local authorities with the ERA providing the opportunity to move further down the road towards the enabling (participatory) role.

IV The response from housing

a) The Welsh context

Wales is divided into geographical areas which have their own particular housing problems (See Welsh House Condition Survey 1988). In addition to problems of poor housing conditions, some authorities also have issues such as second homes and the Welsh language to consider. In most cases the Welsh Office has restricted itself to amending and adapting English legislation to suit the needs of Wales, but this in itself has been significant. For example, the minimum number of houses for an enveloping scheme is lower. The designation of areas as 'rural', thereby allowing authorities to buy back council houses, is much wider and more flexible than in England. The Welsh Office also makes 'top-slice' money available for authorities to buy back second homes. The question of the Welsh language is addressed: authorities have been informed by circular that they may take account of it when developing their structure and local plans. The Welsh Office has also taken financial measures to improve the condition of the housing stock: for example, since 1990 there has been an 'open cheque book' approach to renovation grants.

b) Features of housing in Wales

This section examines the variation in both the content and methods of housing provision in Wales. Six dimensions of the housing service are analysed:

(i) Geographical location - centralised or decentralised

(ii) Internal organisation - functions decentralised or integrated, fragmented or joint departments

(iii) Organisational culture - authorities' perception of those receiving the service

(iv) Housing associations - active or passive approach. Regulatory or *laissez-faire*

(v) Contracting-out - active or passive approach. Regulatory or *laissez-faire*

(vi) Content - provision of a wide or narrow range of housing services e.g 'social-services-style housing'.

i) Geographical location

The housing service in most authorities is still located centrally. Only eight of the thirty-one authorities in our survey have decentralised the housing service. The majority of the eight have decentralised within the last two or three years although two authorities which had been created in 1974 have simply kept their pre-1974 offices open.

The issue of decentralisation has been discussed in many authorities. The reasoning and impetus behind the decentralisation initiatives varied. Only three initiatives appear to have been member-led. Others were led by officers, often aiming to get 'close to the customer'. Other reasons were the retention of the pre-1974 offices, authorities' experience of the Priority Estates Project and the sparsity of the population. Projects planned to overcome the problem of population sparsity include surgeries in rural areas and a mobile housing service. Authorities that had decided against decentralisation had done so because the size of the housing stock or the district did not merit it, or simply because "the costs outweighed the benefits".

ii) Internal organisation

This section examines the allocation of housing functions within the authority. We assess the extent of functional decentralisation in the internal organisation, then examine whether housing responsibilities are fragmented or integrated in a single department.

There did not seem to be a 'typical' type of internal organisation. The extent of decentralisation varied considerably. Only one authority was completely decentralised - each office has its own budgets and responsibility for every housing function. Five authorities have, or plan to have, 'patches' or 'divisions'. These involve one or more officers having responsibility for a range of housing functions in one area, but being based in a central office.

Many housing departments are not fully integrated ie do not encompass the full range of housing-related activities. In two authorities it is not possible to identify a single department with clear responsibility for housing. Only nine authorities have fully integrated departments dealing exclusively with housing. The remaining twelve departments have responsibility for other functions as well as housing. The most common is Environmental Health, although there are examples of departments with responsibility for Finance, Architecture and Leisure.

iii) Organisational culture

This section assesses a key aspect of the 'culture' of housing organisations: the attitude to the people on the receiving end of the service. The view of the majority of authorities is that people who receive a service are 'clients'. These authorities are mainly indifferent to tenant participation. Three interviewees suggested that the lack of tenants associations in their district indicated the relative satisfaction of the tenants. One indicated his scepticism about the value of tenants' views when he said "if you ask people about a service then they are bound to moan and groan about it". Many of the authorities are aware of the concept of 'customer care'. The few that have actually put it into practice have often done so as a response to the 1988 Tenants' Choice legislation. One authority in particular has embraced the concept of customer care by developing a customer care code, which if broken would mean that the customer would be entitled to a payment of ten pounds. Almost one-third of the authorities have surveyed their tenants. Some have plans for annual satisfaction surveys, repairs satisfaction surveys and smaller surveys on specific items. However, in some cases there did not seem to be the will to make changes as a result of these surveys. One interviewee admitted that "in theory the survey has been taken into account but in reality it hasn't".

Only six authorities could be described as having pro-active attitudes to tenant involvement. They encourage and consult the associations through the use of tenant participation officers, small grants, training programmes for tenants and the use of council facilities. One authority provides its tenants associations with an initial grant of one thousand pounds, and an annual grant which is equal to £4.50 for each house in the area that the asssociation covers.

In two authorities, however, tenant involvement is not encouraged. Members felt that it would encroach on their role as "community spokesman". One officer stated that the reason that associations were not encouraged was that ward members for council estates liked everything to go through them. They "liked to have control from the centre".

iv) Housing associations

Enabling authorities are pro-active in their attitudes to housing associations. However, one type of enabling authority emphasises the importance of the market as a self-regulating force. The other seeks to control the market (in this case the housing associations). Traditional authorities might be expected to have a pragmatic view of housing associations and take a passive role.

All authorities have worked with housing associations to some extent, allowing transfers under the Housing Strategy and Investment Programme (HSIP) and giving or selling land and buildings. The reason behind this co-operation is the recognition that it is the only way to maximise their new build supply. Only seven authorities could be described as having a pro-active role. One authority has been involved in so much housing association activity that they have been told by Tai Cymru to hold back any projects over the next couple of years as they have had more than their 'fair share' of the cake. Two authorities are planning to transfer one of their estates to a housing association. The reason behind this is financial rather than political: the authority simply does not have enough money for the extensive repairs needed. None of the authorities fitted into the enabler(market) model. They want more control over the associations and are demanding an increasing amount of information, particularly with regard to relets and nominations. The authorities want to be more interventionist generally. One suggestion that came up frequently was common waiting lists, and pilot schemes on this issue are being discussed in two authorities. One officer took this a step further, suggesting that all social housing should be allocated under one system.

The majority of authorities work with associations but have a more reactive role. Some have worked with associations in a fairly minor way since 1974 but with some difficulties, particularly with the speed of work.

Only one authority has a policy of avoiding collaboration with associations. The authority has actually begun some minor schemes, but only after lengthy and protracted negotiations. One of their councillors was reported as saying that selling council land was "selling our heritage" . An officer in a different authority stated that "some members feel that it is like sitting down to sup with the devil".

Financial restrictions on direct provision have been the main impetus behind the relatively high level of housing association activity. Central government has also persuaded local authorities to work with housing associations through, for example, the HSIP letter.

v) Contracting-out

Both types of enabling authority are active in contracting-out. However, the enabler (market) is likely to have put contracts out to tender before they were forced to and have a *laissez-faire* attitude. The enabler (participatory) authority, on the other hand, is likely to want to control the market in some way. The traditional authority is generally indifferent to compulsive competitive tendering (CCT) and sometimes lacks the split between client and contractor.

Six authorities fitted in to the enabler (participatory) type. Their view was that contracting-out gave them value for money, but they were concerned not to leave everything to market forces. One officer felt that although competitive tendering provides the highest quality and cheapest work, the benefits have to be balanced by the need to keep in mind possible emergencies. This officer had unsuccessfully attempted to get the cleaning of accommodation for elderly people exempted from CCT, as the cleaners provided an important 'social' role and the elderly people needed consistency.

The majority of authorities fall into the traditional category. They are generally indifferent to CCT. Almost all authorities have a client/contractor split but in three the same person is in charge of both sections. Most Direct Service Organisations (DSOs) win all the 'responsive' maintenance and about 50-60 per cent of the 'planned work', and one authority has won as much as 80 per cent in-house. A few authorities have expanded the scope of their work, bidding for contracts from the county and moving into areas such as window-frame manufacture.

Two authorities have side-stepped the legislation on CCT by keeping their workforce below the minimum specified in the legislation. One officer stated that this policy was adopted to "avoid the hassles of CCT". One authority had to tender when the minimum was further reduced and was in the process of extensive reorganisation as a result.

Only two authorities had put contracts out to tender before CCT. The reasons for doing so were practical rather than political. Both had a small housing stock and a small DSO and believed that it was simply easier to contract out much of their work.

vi) Content of service

The type and amount of 'social-service-style' housing varies considerably between authorities. Traditional authorities tend to stick to fairly narrowly defined housing functions whereas others are more innovative. The majority fit the traditional model. All but three authorities have an alarm system for the elderly, but few have gone further than this. Those that have expanded the range of service that they offer have done so fairly extensively. The services that they offer include housing help centres, internal decoration of houses for new tenants who are elderly or disabled, a free furniture shop for tenants, an evening phone debtline, contributions to play leadership schemes, provision of sheltered accommodation, smoke alarms and gas and movement detectors.

Most officers felt they had discretion to provide this type of service but were restricted by general financial controls. Some however felt that it was not their role to provide 'care'.

c) Summary

This section has provided a snapshot of some aspects of housing in Wales. The housing service is in a state of upheaval; authorities are facing challenges and pressures from a changing environment as well as the governments' legislative programme (Stewart 1988). Most are in the process of adapting, but some are doing so quicker than others. Those that have adapted and moved from the 'traditional' housing service have tended to move towards the enabler (participatory) model. Almost one-third of the authorities in our survey have moved in this direction. The majority of authorities in Wales, however, still retain many of the characteristics of a 'traditional' department. The fact that none of the authorities fit into the enabler (market) model is probably a reflection of politics in Wales.

The factors which appear to be significant in the placing of authorities between traditional and enabler (participatory) is the urban/rural split, and the almost totally corresponding split between party political and independent control. In practice, it is impossible to distinguish between these factors because the geographical overlap between them is so close. The authorities that best fitted the enabler (participatory) model were urban and

Labour-controlled. They included all the major urban areas, some of the South Wales valleys and one urban district from North Wales. The remaining authorities fit the traditional model. These include all the rural, independent-controlled authorities.

The extent to which authorities are moving of their own accord or are pushed by the Welsh Office is hard to establish. All interviewees felt, to some extent at least, that they were controlled by central government. As well as financial and legislative restrictions a more 'indistinct' type of control was at work, much of it was conducted informally. One area where it can be seen at work is the HSIP system. Most officers felt that they had to 'play along with the Welsh Office' when putting in their HSIP bid by including bids for their 'pet schemes'. One officer stated that there "was no doubt that they played to rules that the Welsh Office made". A reading of the HSIP letter illustrates the way central government is attempting to push housing departments: towards an enabler (market) orientation as might be expected, but also towards the enabler (participatory) for example, the Housing Options Wales scheme through which authorities can bid for a tenants participation officer for a specified period of time.

Whilst the majority of housing departments in Wales fit into the traditional model almost one-third do not. These departments have moved towards the enabler (participatory) model. The reasons for doing so are varied. Some are moving under their own initiative, but they are also being encouraged by a number of organisations: the Welsh Office, the Institute of Housing, the Local Government Training Board, and the Audit Commission.

V Conclusion

No authority conforms strictly to the ideal type models introduced in the theoretical framework. However, most authorities tend to cluster around either the traditional direct provider model or the enabler (participatory) model. Not only are there variations between authorities, there are also variations within those authorities. These variations exist because of:

• **The existence of statutory and non-statutory service provision**

There is more scope for variation in the non-statutory service areas. Thus in areas such as economic development or leisure we find examples of innovative practices. However, even in areas of statutory service provision there are examples of innovation, such as distance learning, joint ventures and Welsh language teaching.

• The urban/rural split

We found that in housing, for example, all rural authorities can be described as traditional. In other service areas, however, rural authorities have responded to problems by developing new forms of service delivery and working constructively with other bodies. Rural authorities also tend to be politically independent and this may explain differences in approaches to service delivery although it is difficult to disentangle politics and geography.

The strongest commitment to the enabling (participatory) model was found in several of the urban districts. Again, this varied between services. Generally, changes in the scope and methods of service delivery tended to be in response to changes in legislation and in the requirements of central government. For example, few of our authorities would have put their services out to tender without the compulsory requirement. Many local authorities are moving in the direction of the enabling (participatory) model although the pace of change varies between authorities and services. The commitment to changes also varies and depends upon the attitude of professional bodies, the Welsh Office, and the existence of key individuals amongst members and/or officers.

In describing local authorities in Wales as 'traditional' we do not intend to be critical. Our view is that different models will lend themselves to different types of authority and to different services. Indeed, *pragmatic* response to change is a particular feature of local government in Wales.

CHAPTER 5

PROPOSALS FOR REFORM: AN EVALUATION

THE LOCAL GOVERNMENT reorganisation brought in by the 1972 Local Government Act served only to continue the debate on local government in Wales. Almost continuously since 1972 there have been proposals for further radical change. The aim of this chapter is to evaluate the more recent proposals for the reform of local government in Wales. Part I examines the critiques of the current system and the suggestions for reform. Part II evaluates the reform proposals and considers the type of local government system that would best promote democracy and functional performance.

In the following discussion we make no specific assumptions about major political issues in the design of the local government system: that is, the balance at national level between public and private responsibilities; the balance between central and local responsibility for those functions deemed to be appropriately undertaken by the public sector; and the balance between local roles of direct provision and 'enabling' or 'regulating'.

Central policies on these issues are bound to change over time, depending on the ideological preferences of the ruling party. It is therefore pointless to reform local government on the basis of the current fashion at the centre. Rather it is necessary to design a system that is sufficiently flexible to adapt to changing responsibilities and roles. The reform of the local government system in the 1970s produced a uniform and rigid framework that has been overtaken by events in less than twenty years. It is important not to make the same mistake again.

I The proposals
In surveying proposals and attitudes to the reform of local government, it is necessary to consider a range of sources. In recent years Wales Labour Party, the Welsh Social and Liberal

Democrats and Plaid Cymru have formally declared proposals. The local government associations in Wales have their own specific proposals in documents prepared by the Assembly of Welsh Counties (AWC), the Council of Welsh Districts (CWD) and the Wales Association of Community and Town Councils (WACTC). The Conservative Government has also recently initiated a major review of the structure and finance of local government.

The Welsh agenda for reform includes the possibility of an elected body to parallel the Welsh Office, the possible merger of counties and districts, and the role of community and town councils. The debate hardly scratches the surface on deeper questions concerning the purpose and nature of local government, its relationship with citizens and customers, and questions of managerial and political processes that might enhance efficiency, responsiveness and accountability.

a) An elected Welsh assembly

The proposal to establish an elected body for Wales to have some measure of control over the Welsh Office - administrative accountability, financial control or legislative control - is still on the agenda in Wales. This might be considered surprising given that in the devolution referendum in 1979 the Welsh electorate voted by 956,000 to 243,000 against an elected Welsh Assembly. In the North West only 22 per cent of the electorate supported the assembly. In industrial South East Wales only 8 per cent gave support. Nevertheless, a Welsh Assembly is now supported by all the opposition parties and all the local government associations in Wales. The Secretary of State has indicated that the issue is part of the current review of local government but that he remains to be persuaded that an assembly is necessary.

The argument in favour of an assembly is usually related to the existence of the Welsh Office and its associated 'quangos'. This is a substantial tier of government that determines much of the character of social and economic life in Wales. It is claimed that this tier is neither responsive nor accountable to Wales. Its accountability through Welsh Office ministers to Westminster is considered, by critics, to be inadequate. The reformers invariably connect proposals for an elected Assembly for Wales with proposals for local government, even though an elected Assembly to control the Welsh Office would be a reform of central government. Nevertheless it is noted that the Welsh Office is the focus for most of the relationship between central and local government in Wales and its reform could change the character of that relationship. All the reformers appear to accept that an elected Welsh Assembly would create one too many elections in Welsh politics in addition to those related to communities, districts and counties. It is consistently proposed that an elected Assembly would require the elimination of another elected tier of government.

However, there is no necessary connection between the establishment of a Welsh Assembly and the reform of local government. Therefore, it is possible to evaluate proposals for local government reform without assuming any particular framework for the democratic accountability of central government in Wales. In addition, whereas local government reform in the next few years seems probable, the establishment of a Welsh Assembly remains uncertain.

b) The structure and scale of local government

There is widespread agreement that local government in Wales would be improved by the merger of the counties and districts into a single tier of 'most-purpose authorities'. The CWD (1990) argues that single-tier local government would improve accountability, efficiency, co-ordination and public understanding. The Wales Labour Party (1990) argues that single-tier local government would be "more efficient and responsive". The Welsh Social and Liberal Democrats advocate 'most-purpose authorities' in order to "simplify the structure" and "avoid duplication" (1989). Plaid Cymru advocates combining the county and district tiers of government as "the logical consequence of the establishment of a Welsh Senate" (1987). The AWC (1991) admit, a little reluctantly, that "it would not help to add a regional tier without reducing the number of local authority tiers".

Until 1990 the Welsh Office was led by Peter Walker, the architect of the 1972 reforms, and was steadfast in its defence of the existing two-tier structure as the best balance between efficiency and democracy. By the end of 1990 a new Secretary of State for the Environment, Michael Heseltine, had initiated a review of local government in England and a new Secretary of State for Wales, David Hunt, had initiated a parallel review in Wales. The review is incomplete but David Hunt has indicated that he is persuaded of the merits of single-tier local government for at least part of Wales.

This apparent consensus begins to break down when the questions of number and scale of most-purpose authorities are raised. This is not entirely surprising. It will always be difficult to devise a map for local government in Wales if there is any attempt to maintain uniformity of geographical scale and population size. The population is highly concentrated onto the southern and northern coastal fringes. The large mass of Wales is so sparsely concentrated as to make a combination of minimum population size and geographical proximity almost impossible.

Wales Labour Party recommend 25 to 30 most-purpose authorities with an average population of 100,000. The Welsh SLD recommend 24. Nicholas Bennett Welsh Office Minister, identified 16 in a Private Member's Bill. Plaid Cymru and the CWD recommend the current 37 districts. The AWC recommend the current 8 counties. Such an impasse may prove to be a significant deterrent to any future reform.

The problem may be in getting the reformers to identify and discuss not so much the numbers and boundaries but the criteria for determining such structures. Wales Labour Party, for instance, make their recommendation with no indication of the criteria on which it would be based. It is simply noted that it would lead to an average population size of 100,000. In fact, of course, given the nature of population distribution in Wales average population figures are of no relevance. An average of 100,000 might well be achieved through coexistence of Cardiff Council with 300,000 and Radnorshire Council with less than 30,000.

The AWC advocate large-scale authorities based on the current counties and employ Redcliffe Maud-style arguments that a large scale is required to ensure "competence to deliver quality services; professionalism of staff; and the ability to take a strategic view".

This proposition is asserted rather than argued. It is not admitted that in advocating the current boundaries they are recommending Mid Glamorgan with over 500,000 population and Powys with only 100,000. If scale is the criterion for structuring local government, can both these local authorities be appropriate? The CWD specifically rejects scale as the relevant criterion. The identification of minimum scale, it argues, is related to the goal of an organisation which is self-sufficient in the resources needed for service delivery. The CWD appear willing to accept that the ideal local authority will gain and control a range of its required resources from the market-place and through joint agencies. It uses the fashionable concept of an 'enabling' authority to justify the existence of small-scale local authorities. In contrast to minimum scale as the appropriate criterion the CWD recommends the criterion of 'community' and on this basis recommends a flexible local government map that accommodates relatively large populations with relatively small populations:

> The only valid principle to guide the specification of boundaries for a local authority is that of 'sense of community'. In an urban setting that community sense of common interest, common purpose and common allegiance may cover a large population. In a rural setting, depending on mobility patterns, the appropriate boundaries might cover relatively extensive area but a relatively small population. (CWD, 1990, p5)

Since 1974 there have been over 750 community and town councils in Wales. In Gwynedd, Dyfed and Powys there is comprehensive coverage by such councils. In other, more urban, areas there is only partial coverage. These councils have limited powers to provide some local services but no statutory responsibility to do so. They have the 'expressive' role of identifying local needs and communicating them to other authorities. All the reform proposals support the continuation of these councils and even an enhancement of their role. In this there is a paradox. The reformers extol the virtues of single-tier local government and yet propose an additional tier as a footnote to their proposals. The real nature of the proposals is the continuation of a multi-tier system but with little thought thus far given to the role of the tier which is closest to the people of Wales. Griffiths and Lawton (1990) have explored the possibilities for this tier of government. They note the great diversity of community and town councils in Wales. A few represent towns of over 30,000 people. Most represent rural villages with less than 2,000 population. It is likely to be concluded that there should be substantial diversity in the roles undertaken by these councils. All have a role in providing an alternative means of identifying and articulating local demands. Some could usefully act as agents for a larger tier of local government in the delivery of services. Some of the larger community councils may claim statutory powers and responsibilities in a legislative framework that should facilitate a local diversity for the structure of local government.

II Evaluation

The reform proposals can be evaluated on the basis of two criteria: the level of democracy in local government and the functional performance of local authorities in carrying out their responsibilities. These criteria are central requirements of any political system: policies should reflect public preferences and have the desired results at minimum cost. Democracy and functional performance can be used as yardsticks to compare the reform proposals with each other and with the existing local government system.

a) Democracy

In this section we use the following democratic principles to evaluate the proposals for local government reform: the extent of public representation in decision-making through the electoral process; the opportunity for direct public participation in policy-making; the capacity of local authorities for responsiveness to public demands; and the dispersal of political power within and across areas.

i) Structure

The consensus in favour of a system of unitary authorities seems unlikely to enhance the level of democracy in the local government system. The removal of a tier of local government is likely to reduce the number of councillors and therefore reduce the quantity of elected representation in local government. In addition, representation is based on a particular geographical location. Undoubtedly, there are interests common to one area. There are particular Welsh concerns that have no equivalent in England (for example, the Welsh language) and there are different interests within different parts of Wales. However, to define a natural community of interests based upon a single area is sometimes difficult. Citizens may belong to work communities or social communities with different geographical boundaries. The reform of local government should reflect this diversity by providing for representation at different tiers with different geographical constituencies. Opportunities for participation may also be more limited in a unitary system than in a two-tier system: the existence of a second tier provides an alternative channel of access to policy decisions.

The responsiveness of the local government system is likely to be reduced by the introduction of a single-tier system. It may be argued that unitary authorities enhance responsiveness to public preferences because priorities can be determined across a range of services. However, in a unitary system the balance between services is decided directly by politicians and officials - the influence of the public is indirect at best. By contrast, if there is more than one tier then the public may be able to influence directly the balance between groups of services. For example, in the existing structure of local government there is the possibility of voting for higher spending on district services and lower spending on county services.

Finally, a unitary system may concentrate power in local government. Part of the rationale for the existence of democratic local government is to disperse political power between the centre and the localities and so reflect the plurality of interests in society. Local government can act as a buffer against the potential 'tyranny' of central government. However, the potential for overbearing power also exists within local areas. A two-tier system can help to provide a safeguard against local despotism.

ii) Scale

It has often been argued in debates on local government reform that small local authorities are inherently more democratic than large local authorities (Dearlove, 1979). The empirical evidence on the relationship between size and participation is mixed (Newton, 1982). However, smaller authorities are likely to increase the level of public representation and to increase the dispersal of power: a system of small authorities may lead to fewer electors per councillor, and to more 'points of decision' in the local government system.

The most important democratic advantage of small authorities is probably their capacity for responsiveness. Governments can more readily be responsive where there is public agreement on the policies that are required. Larger local authorities are more likely to contain a greater variety of interests and viewpoints, and greater disagreement on policy choices. Thus smaller local government units may find it easier to match policies to public demands. Smaller-scale authorities may also facilitate direct communication between citizens and politicians. It is important to note that larger authorities can achieve some of the responsiveness of smaller units if services are decentralised or if citizens are directly involved in the actual design and delivery of the services. Nevertheless, the 'welfare loss' from a mismatch between policy decisions and public demands is likely to rise with scale.

b) Functional performance

Terms such as 'efficiency' and 'quality' are often used in proposals for local government reform, but they are seldom clearly defined. This vagueness means that it is difficult to identify precisely the intended impact of changes to structure and scale. The broad concept of 'functional performance' may be defined as including economy in the purchase of service inputs, such as materials and staff; efficiency in the use of these inputs to produce outputs and effectiveness, in other words the extent to which service provision has the desired results. Will the proposed reforms to structure and scale enhance the achievement of any or all these aspects of functional performance?

i) Structure

It is claimed that the concentration of all major service responsibilities in 'unitary' authorities would improve service co-ordination and remove service duplication, thereby increasing efficiency. However, the exact source and likely magnitude of the cost savings are not clearly specified in the reform proposals. The argument for a single tier of local government may rest in part on a nostalgia for the county boroughs in the pre-1974 local government system. For example, Alexander (1982, p 63) has stated that the county boroughs were "the most effective unit of local government in the unreformed system, perhaps the best institution of sub-national government ever developed in a unitary state". However, there is no direct evidence on the relative functional performance of county boroughs and the authorities that replaced them in 1974. Even if comparable figures were available, it would be very difficult to isolate the impact of structural change from changes in the environment and responsibilities of local government since 1974. The argument for 'most-purpose' authorities also reflects the power struggle in the local government system: it is no surprise that the AWC and CWD have advocated a single tier based on the counties and districts respectively.

Some insight on the relationship between structure and efficiency can be gained from empirical analyses of the local government system in the USA, where there has been a long debate on the relative merits of 'consolidated' and 'fragmented' local government systems. In a consolidated structure responsibilities are concentrated in single units. In a fragmented structure responsibilities are spread across units which provide discrete groups of services or a single service. In the USA local government structures vary both across and within states. This diversity facilitates the analysis of the impact of structures on performance. The empirical evidence generally indicates that a consolidated local government structure is associated with higher costs, and that a fragmented local government structure is associated with lower costs (for example, Mehay, 1984; Schneider, 1986). Such evidence may not transfer directly to local government in the UK, but it does illustrate the potential drawback of concentrating all major service responsibilities in a single authority.

There are several reasons why costs may be higher if all services are provided by a single local government unit in each area. First, a unitary authority has a monopoly on the local tax base. By contrast, if there is more than one tier of authorities then they must compete for tax revenue, and this can act as a spur to efficiency. Second, some overlap in service responsibilities between tiers may provide flexibility to develop functions at the more cost-effective level. Third, while councillors and officers may be irritated by 'conflict' between tiers, each level may be a source of scrutiny on the other and may threaten to expose 'extravagance'.

Thus the case is unproven that the removal of one tier of local government will in itself enhance functional performance. In addition, it is possible that the concentration of powers in unitary authorities will drive up costs because of the loss of 'internal competition' in the local government system.

ii) Scale

Part of the rationale for the 1974 reforms was that larger authorities were required to achieve 'economies of scale' and to provide specialised services. Such arguments have recently been repeated by the AWC. Is there an optimal population size for local authorities? Does size make any difference to functional performance?

The argument that a minimum scale is required to provide specialised services may have been valid in an era of 'self-sufficient' local authorities. However, this argument carries less weight in the context of mixed modes of service provision. Scale is much less relevant to specialisation if authorities can purchase services as required rather than maintaining a standing army of 'in-house' professionals. Chapter 4 gives examples of small rural authorities ensuring service provision by acting in an 'enabling' role.

If there are scale economies in local government then the cost per unit of provision should fall as the quantity of provision rises. There has been much research on this issue, but the evidence is inconclusive (Newton, 1982). This may be because the quality of the evidence is generally poor. Most of the analyses of scale-effects have tested the relationship between spending per capita and population size. These measures are weak proxies for unit costs and quantity of provision respectively. Thus there may be either economies or diseconomies of scale, but such measures are unlikely to reveal either effect.

In the context of the available evidence, then, it would be unwise to place the economic benefits of scale at the centre of arguments for local government reform. Even if there are scale-effects the optimal population size is likely to depend on the package of services to be delivered and the geographical scale of the area. Such considerations imply diversity rather than uniformity in the appropriate scale of local government units.

c) Implications
The above analysis suggests that the following arrangements are likely to promote democracy and functional performance in local government.

i) More than one tier of authorities
If service responsibilities are concentrated in a single tier of authorities then democracy may be restricted: opportunities for participation and representation are limited, and there is no alternative local democratic channel if the door of the 'one-stop shop' is unwelcoming or closed. Functional performance is also likely to be lower in a single-tier structure because of the absence of internal competition in the local government system.

ii) Small-scale authorities
Functional performance does not appear to be affected significantly by scale. However, the greater homogeneity of preferences in small communities enhances the democratic capacity of smaller units of local government to match policies with public demands. A disadvantage of small-scale authorities

may be that the scope for redistribution is limited, assuming that local authority boundaries separate poor communities from rich communities. However, redistribution may in any case be better achieved through central grants than through intra-community transfers.

iii) Diversity in structure and scale

Previous local government re-organisations and most of the reform proposals involve a uniform and standardised local government system in Wales. Differences in local circumstances, experience and preferences suggest that democracy and functional performance may be maximised by variations in the division of tasks between local government tiers, and by variations in population size.

None of the current reform packages explicitly advocates a local government system which is generally two-tier, small-scale and variable between areas. However, there are elements within the reform proposals which, if combined, could form the basis for such a system.

First, the CWD, AWC and the WACTC are agreed that greater powers should be bestowed on community councils. If the transfer of powers was substantial then a two-tier system would operate, assuming that an upper tier of either the county or the districts remained. There has, as yet, been insufficient consideration of the variety of roles that might be performed by community and town councils. Unless this is clarified during the reform process, it is likely to remain confused in the practice of local government. Such confusion would undermine public understanding, involvement and support for local government.

Second, the CWD proposals envisage the abolition of the counties. The view of the Conservative government is also that the introduction of a single-tier system will be based on the districts in most areas. This would substantially reduce the average population and the geographical size of local government units. If the community councils also had more powers, then the level of decentralisation would be far greater still.

Third, the government has suggested that there should be an element of local variability in the reform of local government:

local 'consultation' will be used to decide whether to retain the county or the districts (or both) in each area. This introduces a welcome element of local choice in the reform process. However, local choice and variability could be taken much further in decisions concerning structure and scale. For example, community councils could be given the power to decide whether they wish to take over some of the functions of the upper-tier council. Local choice would be further extended if the distribution of functions was also decided by referendum, initially at the same time as the establishment of the new system. Subsequent referenda at reasonable intervals could be used to decide whether to acquire further functions, or to return functions to the upper-tier authority. The existence of local choice to switch functions between tiers would give expression to the criteria of both democracy and functional performance, not least because each tier would be subject to a 'competitive threat' from the other tier if it failed to reflect public preferences and offer cost-effective services. At the same time local choice would facilitate local accountability.

III Conclusion

Various proposals to reform the local government system have been put forward by local authority associations and political parties in Wales. Specific elements of many of these proposals offer an improvement over the current system on criteria of democracy and functional performance. Our analysis of the reform proposals suggests that the general direction of reform should be towards a two-tier structure, small-scale authorities and geographical variability in the local government system.

The Conservative government has recently proposed a reform of local government that places some emphasis on local choice. Local communities are to be allowed to retain either the county or the districts, and Wales is to be allowed to follow a separate path from England. It can only be hoped that the government's new-found commitment to local diversity is sustained during the reform process. Once the general outline of a new system is developed, the next stage should be to consider the map of Wales piece by piece. There needs to be a debate about local government not in Wales as a whole, but in areas such as the North West, in the rural middle and in the industrial valleys. In each case the debate needs to include participants from district, county and community councils, their citizens and organisations such as Chambers of Commerce and Trade Unions. Each debate might come to very different conclusions.

But if local government is to be local in its operations, should it not be local in the creation of its institutions? If local government is about maintaining a pluralistic diversity, should not that diversity be apparent in its very structures and scale?

CHAPTER 6

CONCLUSIONS

IN THIS FINAL CHAPTER we consider the implications of our research for the future of local government in Wales.

In Chapter 2 it was argued that Welsh local government is not simply a spoke in the wheel of the larger English system. Rather, local government in Wales is sufficiently distinct to constitute a system in its own right. The development of this system owes much to the establishment of the Welsh Office in the 1960s, which has led to separate processes of central-local relations and to the formation of separate Welsh policy communities. Nevertheless, it may be argued that the current constitutional position of the Welsh Office is an obstacle to policy decisions that would more fully reflect local preferences in Wales. Greater responsiveness to public demands might be achieved if the Welsh Office were to be democratically accountable through a Welsh Assembly. However, this argument overlooks the threat that a Welsh Assembly might pose to local democracy. The establishment of an Assembly might devolve power from London to Wales; but if the Assembly takes over responsibilities from local authorities then it will also centralise power *within* Wales. This would be a difficult balance to strike. The choice, if it ever arises, would test the commitment of the Welsh people to genuine decentralisation.

In Chapter 3 it was shown that there has been some reduction in local autonomy in recent years. Local government as a whole has been pushed in the general direction desired by the centre, but central government has had little impact on local policy diversity. It seems certain that central government will continue to set and enforce objectives for the local government system. Central politicians hold local authorities 'responsible' for delivering some of their manifesto commitments. The only ways to remove this constraint on local autonomy are for national politicians to renounce their powers over important public services, or for local authorities to retain only trivial responsibilities. In the absence of these unlikely outcomes, local and central government must simply live with an inescapable tension in their relationship. However, if local authorities must endure being 'pushed around' by central government, then the centre might ease the burden by showing a greater tolerance of variations in local policies. As the evidence in Chapter 3 indicates, the centre has wasted a good deal of time and effort trying to constrain local policy differences. Central policy-makers may never learn to love diversity, but they may be persuaded that attempts to curb it are costly and mostly futile.

In Chapter 4 it was concluded that local authorities in Wales have, in general, proved reluctant to relinquish their role of direct service provider. Some recent movement towards an enabling role has occurred as a result of central policies and fiscal pressure. Some authorities, particularly in more rural areas, have taken a flexible approach to service provision for many years. In other areas it has been necessary to retain direct responsibility for services because of the absence of external contractors or voluntary organisations with an interest in the work. In addition, central dogma should not be allowed to obscure the fact that direct provision may offer the best response to local problems in some services and some areas. However, the results of our survey suggest that there is more scope for Welsh local authorities to experiment with mixed methods of service provision. For the public to secure maximum benefit from the local government system it is necessary not only for the centre to tolerate local diversity, but also for local councils to promote diversity in the pattern of service provision. This point is reinforced by the analysis in Chapter 5 which suggests that small-scale authorities may be best placed to maximise democracy and functional performance. If local government reform does produce a reduction in the average size of local authorities then a greater emphasis on enabling and collaborative roles will be required.

Our evaluation of proposals for local government reform in Chapter 5 concentrated on the 'Welsh agenda' of structure and scale. There has been an assumption that the future reform of local government in Wales will lead to a single tier of authorities and that this is beneficial in itself. Our evidence is that there are inherent benefits in a multi-tier system of local government.

Moreover, we have identified that the reform proposals do incorporate more than one tier when the role of community and town councils is identified. Change in Wales is likely to involve some merger of districts and counties on a scale smaller than the present counties. If the new authorities better approximate the perceptions of communities within Wales, this reduction in scale is likely to be beneficial. In addition, there is likely to be a more local tier of community and town councils. This additional tier of government can add to the participative potential, the effective communication of demands and the pluralism of Welsh government. However, there has been insufficient consideration of the variety and diversity of roles that might be performed by community and town councils. It is essential that this issue is clarified during the reform process.

It is impossible to conclude our report without considering the issue that has dominated the wider local government agenda for almost twenty years: finance. For the last decade the Conservative government has argued correctly that local accountability is weakened if local taxpayers bear only a small proportion of the costs of local government. This argument has recently been cast aside by the decision to substitute VAT revenue for poll tax revenue. The increase in central funding blurs considerably the focus of local accountability, especially in Wales where in some areas local taxes will cover less than 10 per cent of local service costs.

It is to be hoped that over the next few years grants will again be allowed to decline as a proportion of local spending. However, it will be difficult to increase the level of local taxes unless the basis of taxation is perceived as equitable. In addition, local authorities require a tax base that is at least as buoyant as that enjoyed by central government, otherwise central government's share of total tax revenues is bound to increase over time. The ending of this 'fiscal discrimination' against local government should be a key part of any package of reforms.

All those who participate and take an interest in local government in Wales should welcome the opportunity provided by the reform debate to reaffirm that local government is about responsiveness, accountability and is, above all, local in character.

REFERENCES

Alexander, A (1982), *The Politics of Local Government in the United Kingdom* (London, Longman)

Assembly of Welsh Counties (1991), *Review of Structures, Finance and Functions of Local Government in Wales* (Cardiff, Wales Labour Party)

Ball, I (1980), 'Urban Investment Controls in Britain' in D E Ashford (ed), *National Resources and Urban Policy* (New York, Methuen)

Balsom, D (1987), 'Ceredigion District Council ' in Elcock, H, and G Jordan, *Learning from Local Authority Budgeting* (Aldershot, Avebury)

Bennet, R J (1980), *The Geography of Public Finance* (London, Methuen)

Boaden, N (1971), *Urban Policy Making* (Cambridge, Cambridge University Press)

Boyne, G A (1989), 'Local Tax Equalisation in England: An Empirical Analysis', *Government and Policy*, 7, 245-59

Boyne, G A (1990), 'Central Grants and Local Policy Variation', *Public Administration*, 68, 207-35

Boyne, G A and J Law (1991), 'Accountability and Local Authority Annual Reports: The case of Welsh District Councils', *Financial Accountability and Management*, 7 (3)

Bramley, G, J Le Grand and W Low (1989), 'How far is the Poll Tax a Community Charge? The Implications of Service Usage Evidence', *Policy and Politics*, 17, 187-205

Bulpitt, J (1983), *Territory and Power in the UK* (Manchester, Manchester University Press)

Bulpitt, J (1989), 'Walking Back to Happiness? Conservative Party Governments and Elected Local Authorities in the 1980s', in

Crouch and Marquand, *The New Centralism*

Butcher, H, I Law, R Leach and M Mullard (1989), *Local Government and Thatcherism* (London, Routledge)

Cabinet Office (1989), *Public Bodies* (London, HMSO)

Clark, G (1984), 'A Theory of Local Autonomy' *Annals of the Association of American Geographers*, 74, 195-208

Clarke, M and J Stewart (1988), *The Enabling Council* (Luton, LGTB)

Clarke, M and J Stewart (1989), *Challenging Old Assumptions: The Enabling Council Takes Shape* (Luton, LGTB)

Council of Welsh Districts (1990), *Closer to the People of Wales* (Cardiff, CWD)

Cross, C and S Bailey (1986), *Cross on Local Government Law* (London, Sweet and Maxwell)

Crouch, C and D Marquand eds (1989), *The New Centralism* (Oxford, Basil Blackwell)

Danziger, J (1978), *Making Budgets* (London, Sage)

Dearlove, J (1979), *The Reorganisation of British Local Government* (Cambridge, CUP)

Duncan, S and M Godwin (1988), *The Local State and Uneven Development* (Cambridge, Polity Press)

Foster, C, R Jackman and R Pearlman (1980), *Local Government Finance in a Unitary State* (London, George Allen & Unwin)

Foulkes, D, J Jones and R A Wilford (1983), *The Welsh Veto, The Wales Act 1978 and the Referendum* (Cardiff, University of Wales Press)

Goldsmith, M and E Page (1987), 'Britain' in Page and Goldsmith (eds) *Central and Local Government Relations* (London, Sage)

Goodin, R and J Le Grand (1987), *Not Only The Poor* (London, George Allen & Unwin)

Griffiths, P (1987), 'Mid Glamorgan County Council', in Elcock, H, and G Jordan *Learning from Local Authority Budgeting* (Aldershot, Avebury)

Griffiths, P and A Lawton (1990), *Community Councils in Wales* (Wales Association of Community and Town Councils)

Hartley, O (1971), 'The Relationship Between Central And Local Authorities', *Public Administration*, 49, 439-56

HMI Report (1988), *Some Aspects of Educational Provision in Wales 1986-87* Welsh Office

Houlihan, B (1988), *Housing Policy and Central-Local Relations* (Aldershot, Avebury)

Heady, B (1978), *Housing Policy in the Developed Economy* (London, Croom Helm)

Jones, B (1986), 'Welsh Local Government: A Blueprint for Regionalism', *Local Government Studies*, 12 no 5, 61-74

Layfield (1976), *Layfield Committee of Enquiry*, Cmnd 6453 (London, HMSO)

Le Grand, J (1982), *The Strategy of Equality* (London, George Allen & Unwin)

Leonard, M (1988), *The 1988 Education Act: A Tactical Guide for Schools* (Oxford, Blackwell)

Local Government Commission for Wales (1963), *Report and Proposals for Wales* (London, HMSO)

Loughlin, M (1986), *Local Government in the Modern State* (London, Sweet & Maxwell)

Madgwick, P J and M James (1979), *Government by Consultation: The case of Wales* (Centre for the Study of Public Policy, University of Strathclyde)

Madgwick, P and P Rawkins (1982), 'The Welsh Language in the Policy Process' in P Madgwick and R Rose (ed) *The Territorial Dimension in United Kingdom Politics* (London, Macmillan)

Mehay, S (1984), 'The Effect of Governmental Structure on Special District Expenditures', *Public Choice* 44, 339-48

Morgan, K O (1981), *Rebirth of a Nation, Wales 1880-1980* (Oxford, Clarendon Press)

National Audit Office (1989), *Welsh Office: Financial Management* (London HMSO)

Newton, K (1982), 'Is Small Really So Beautiful? Is Big Really So Ugly? Size, Effectiveness and Democracy in Local Government', *Political Studies*, 30, 190-206

Newton, K and T Karran (1985), *The Politics of Local Expenditure* (London, Macmillan)

Osmond, J (1985), 'The Dynamic of Institutions', in Osmond, J (ed), *The National Question Again* (Llandysul, Gomer Press)

Page, E (1980), 'The Measurement of Central Control', *Political Studies* 28, 117-20

Page, E (1982), 'The Value of Local Autonomy' *Local Government Studies*, 8, no. 4, 21-42

Rhodes, G (1981), *Inspectorates in British Government* (London, George Allen & Unwin)

Rhodes, R (1985), *The National World of Local Government* (London, Allen & Unwin)

Rhodes, R (1988), *Beyond Westminster and Whitehall* (London, Unwin Hyman)

Robson, W A (1968), *Local Government in Crisis* (London, George Allen & Unwin, 2nd Edition)

Sharpe, L J and K Newton (1984), *Does Politics Matter?* (Oxford, Clarendon)

Schneider, M (1986), 'Fragmentation and the Growth of Local Government' *Public Choice*, 48, 255-63

Smith, P (1988), 'Assessing Competition Among Local Authorities in England and Wales', *Financial Accountability and Management*, 4, 235-51

Stewart, J (1988), *A New Management for Housing Departments*, Local Government Training Board

Stoker, G (1988), *The Politics of Local Government* (London, Macmillan)

Travers, T (1989), 'The Threat to the Autonomy of Elected Local Government' in Crouch and Marquand, *The New Centralism*

Wales Labour Party (1990), *The Future of Local Government in Wales* (Cardiff, Wales Labour Party)

Welsh Social and Liberal Democrats (1989), *Enhancing Democracy and the Revival of Local Government* (Newport SWLD)

Welsh Office (1967), *Local Government in Wales*, Cmnd 3340 (London, HMSO)

Welsh Office (1970), *Local Government Reorganisation: Glamorgan and Monmouthshire*, Cmnd 4310 (London, HMSO)

Welsh Office (1971), *The Reform of Local Government in Wales*, Consultative document

Welsh Office (1988), *1986 Welsh House Condition Survey* (Welsh Office)

Widdicombe (1986), *The Conduct of Local Authority Business, Report of the Committee of Inquiry into the conduct of Local Authority Business*, Cmnd 9797 (London, HMSO)

Williams, G A (1985), *When Was Wales?* (Black Raven Press)

APPENDIX 1: TABLES

Table 1: Percentage variation of Welsh figures from English figures (per capita)

	1979/80	1981/2	1984/5	1987/8	1990/1
Total net current expenditure	+21	+18	+21	+21	+20
Service expenditures: [1]					
Education	+ 12	+15	+18	+13	+ 15
Libraries	+2	-1	+1	-1	-1
Personal social services	+20	+19	+16	+12	+23
Police	+5	+7	+9	+10	+8
Fire	+18	+15	+19	+19	+13
Rate subsidy to Housing Revenue	+102	+97	+52	+557	-
Highways	+33	+46	+32	+42	+30
Transport (revenue support)	+56	+28	+17	+38	-
Planning	(+38	(+68	+15	+10	-
Economic development	(+38	(+68	+357	+405	+230
Refuse collection	+8	+6	+10	+8	+8
Environmental health	+41	+39	+48	+43	+22
Recreation	+66	+63	+81	+62	+48
Museums, galleries and theatres	-	-	+2	+5	-
Expenditure 'need'	-	+16	+18	+20	+22
Central grants	+45	+48	+63	+90	+122[2]

Table 2: Central grants as a percentage of total net current expenditure

	1979/80	1981/2	1984/5	1987/8	1990/1[2]
Wales	72	71	69	63	56
England	60	55	51	40	31

Notes

[1] Actuals, 1979/80 to 1987/8; Estimates 1990/1
[2] Excludes national non-domestic rates
- data unavailable
Sources : *Local Government Comparative Statistics, Finance and General Statistics*
(London, CIPFA, annual)

Table 3: Real change in Welsh local government spending, 1974/5 to 1988/9 (1974/5 = 100)

	Gross Revenue Expenditure (1)	Net Revenue Expenditure (2)	Gross Capital Expenditure (3)
1974/5	100	100	100
1975/6	102.3	105.3	80.0
1976/7	102.2	103.6	69.3
1977/8	98.7	97.3	50.5
1978/9	103.5	98.9	53.6
1979/80	104.5	96.6	53.2
1980/1	108.5	101.9	50.6
1981/2	105.8	97.9	44.6
1982/3	106.3	96.5	57.2
1983/4	109.8	93.4	63.5
1984/5	112.5	96.0	53.5
1985/6	111.8	97.0	48.5
1986/7	117.2	103.2	54.7
1987/8	121.3	107.4	62.1
1988/9	124.6	108.5	62.6

Notes
(1) Funded from grants, rates and other income
(2) Funded from grants and rates only
(3) Excludes 'negative' capital expenditure (income from capital receipts)

Sources: spending figures from *Welsh Local Government Financial Statistics* (Cardiff, Welsh Office, annual); figures adjusted to constant price base using monthly RPI changes from *Economic Trends, No 15* (London, HMSO, 1990)

Table 4: Direct provision: local authorities as employers and landlords

	Full-time equivalent staff (thousands)	Housing stock (thousands)	Sales as % of stock	New dwellings completed
1974	—	279	—	3,046
1975	123.7	288	0.02	7,332
1976	126.8	295	0.09	6,864
1977	124.9	302	0.15	6,575
1978	125.5	306	0.31	4,111
1979	128.0	308	0.41	3,010
1980	127.9	306	0.70	3,493
1981	125.1	293	2.88	3,370
1982	122.7	278	5.61	1,771
1983	123.9	271	3.37	1,543
1984	123.4	267	2.15	1,997
1985	121.8	262	2.14	992
1986	120.9	258	2.09	744
1987	120.4	253	2.22	810
1988	121.4	244	3.81	793
1989	121.9	232	5.25	566

Sources: Staffing:*Welsh Local Government Financial Statistics*, (Cardiff, Welsh Office, annual); Housing: *Welsh Housing Statistics,* (Cardiff, Welsh Office, annual)

Table 5: Charges, subsidies and redistribution (1975/6 = 100)

	Income from fees and charges rate fund services (1)	Rate fund subsidies to trading services	Rate fund contribution to housing revenue account
1975/6	100	100	100
1976/7	110	81	72
1977/8	113	88	68
1978/9	131	91	76
1979/80	133	76	62
1980/1	131	67	69
1981/2	144	79	53
1982/3	147	69	50
1983/4	151	53	34
1984/5	157	50	23
1985/6	159	48	18
1986/7	163	48	18
1987/8	166	47	26
1988/9	170	43	31

(1) Excludes housing and trading services

Source: *Welsh Local Government Financial Statistics* (Cardiff, Welsh Office, annual)

Table 6: Welsh local authority spending and central assessment of spending 'needs'. Expenditure as a percentage of GREA and SSA (1990/1)

	Mean	Coefficient of variation	Minimum	Maximum
(Counties)				
1981/2	+4	0.05	-1 (Gwynedd)	−15 (West Glam)
1982/3	+5	0.04	+1 (South Glam)	−12 (West Glam)
1983/4	+3	0.04	-1 (Dyfed)	+10 (West Glam)
1984/5	+2	0.04	-2 (Dyfed)	+8 (West Glam)
1985/6	+1	0.04	-3 (South Glam)	+5 (West Glam)
1986/7	+5	0.04	+1 (Gwynedd)	+14 (Clwyd)
1987/8	+2	0.02	-1 (Gwynedd)	+6 (West Glam)
1988/9	+3	0.02	-1 (Gwynedd)	+8 (West Glam)
1989/90	+2	0.03	-2 (Powys)	+7 (West Glam)
1990/1	+4	0.03	+1 (Powys)	+9 (Clwyd)
Districts				
1981/2	+8	0.16	-18 (Cardiff)	+44 (Blaenau Gwent)
1982/3	+3	0.15	-25 (M'gomery)	+35 (Blaenau Gwent)
1983/4	-3	0.16	-32 (Dinefwr)	+47 (Arfon)
1984/5	+1	0.10	-23 (Dinefwr)	+19 (Port Talbot)
1985/6	-3	0.13	-28 (Radnor)	+30 (Blaenau Gwent)
1986/7	+8	0.09	-12 (Dinefwr)	+23 (Port Talbot)
1987/8	+1	0.09	-17 (Cardiff)	+15 (Port Talbot)
1988/9	=	0.09	-19 (Neath)	+16 (Port Talbot)
1989/90	=	0.09	-18 (Dinefwr)	+20 (Meirionnydd)
1990/1	+15	0.15	-14 (S Pembs)	+74 (Dwyfor)

Source: Derived from *Finance and General Statistics* (London, CIPFA, annual)

Table 7: Welsh county policy variations

All services:	1979/80	1980/1-1983/4	1984/5-1988/9
Net spending per capita	C.10	0.08	0.05
Capital spending per capita	-	0.27	0.27
Full-time staff per capita	0.10	0.09	0.09
Part-time staff per capita	0.05	0.07	0.08
Social services			
Net spending per capita	0.12	0.11	0.12
Fieldwork staff per capita	0.20	0.18	0.19
Administrative staff per capita	0.16	0.18	0.19
Home-help contact hours per 'over-65'	0.29	0.27	0.32
Spending per elderly resident in care	0.07	0.08	0.10
Police			
Net spending per capita	0.05	0.09	0.09
Officers per capita	0.04	0.06	0.09
Civilians per capita	0.15	0.20	0.21
Fire			
Net spending per capita	0.05	0.07	0.06
Full-time officers per capita	0.29	0.30	0.32
Part-time staff per capita	0.96	0.96	0.94
Control room staff per capita	0.17	0.17	0.18
Highways			
Net spending per capita	0.37	0.44	0.46
Principal roads, maintenance spending per km	0.49	0.45	0.54
Non-principal roads, maintenance spending per km	0.37	0.37	0.41
Libraries			
Net spending per capita	0.21	0.20	0.15
Staff per capita	0.24	0.19	0.13
Book issues per capita	-	0.16	0.15
Transport			
Revenue support per capita	0.37	0.33	0.36
Planning			
Net spending per capita	0.18	0.19	0.16

Notes
1 - Indicates no data available

Source: *Local Government Comparative Statistics; Capital Expenditure and Debt Financing Statistics* (London, CIPFA, annual)

Table 8: Variations in Welsh county education policies

Coefficients of variation

	1979/80 [1]	1980/1-1983/4	1984/5-1988/9
Net spending per capita	0.07	0.07	0.08
Capital spending per capita	—	0.35	0.34
Nursery and primary [2]			
Gross spending per pupil	0.10	0.09	0.08
Primary pupil/teacher ratio	0.09	0.09	0.09
Nursery pupil/teacher ratio	0.07	0.10	0.15
Secondary			
Gross spending per pupil	0.07	0.07	0.07
Pupil/teacher ratio	0.03	0.03	0.04
Spending on books and equipment per pupil	0.12	0.10	0.14
Non-advanced further education			
Net spending per capita	0.12	0.16	0.22

Notes
(1) Average 1976/7 to 1979/90 for pupil/teacher ratios
(2) No nursery schools are provided directly by Gwynedd or Powys

Sources: *Local Government Comparative Statistics; Capital Expenditure and Debt Financing Statistics; Education Statistics, Actuals* (all London, CIPFA, annual); *Statistics of Education in Wales* (Cardiff, Welsh Office, annual)

Table 9: Welsh district policy variations

All services	1979/80	1980/1- 1983/4	1984/5- 1988/9
Net spending per capita	0.23	0.21	0.25
Capital spending per capita	-	0.37	0.38
Full-time staff per capita	0.28	0.27	0.25
Part-time staff per capita	0.42	0.44	0.42
Refuse collection			
Net spending per capita	0.22	0.22	0.24
Staff per capita	0.37	0.35	0.30
Cost per tonne collected	-	0.42	0.42
Refuse disposal			
Net spending per capita	0.58	0.55	0.54
Staff per capita	0.67	0.62	0.69
Cost per tonne disposed of	-	0.54	0.59
Recreation			
Net spending per capita	0.51	0.51	0.47
Revenue/cost ratio	0.59	0.49	0.48
Environmental health			
Net spending per capita	0.30	0.30	0.25
Transport			
Concessionary fares, net spending per capita	0.51	0.53	0.55
Rate collection			
Cost per hereditament	-	0.28	0.26
Staff per hereditament	-	0.28	0.23
Trading services			
Revenue/cost ratio, all	0.44	0.47	0.41
Revenue/cost ratio, trade and industrial estates	1.14	1.15	0.50
Museums, galleries and theatres			
Net spending per capita	-	0.98	1.2
Planning			
Net spending per capita	0.50	0.61	0.54

Note:

1. - indicates no data available

Source: *Local Government Comparative Statistics, Capital Expenditure and Debt Financing Statistics* (London, CIPFA, annual)

Table 10: Variations in Welsh district housing policies

| | Coefficients of variation | | |
	1974-79	1980-83	1984-89
Percentage of new building by council	0.58	0.85	1.11
Capital spending per capita	-	0.42	0.47
Percentage of stock sold	2.55	0.83	0.38
Improvement grants per dwelling (1)	0.45	0.58	0.71
Rent levels	0.11	C.11	0.13
Percentage rate subsidy to housing revenue account	0.35	0.66	1.20

Note:
(1) Figures for 1979 only in first column

Source: *Welsh Housing Statistics* (Cardiff, Welsh Office, annual); *Housing Revenue Account Statistics Actuals, Housing Rents Statistics, Capital Expenditure and Debt Financing Statistics* (London, CIPFA, annual)

Table 11: Political autonomy - Labour control and policy outputs (1)

(a) Counties

	Periods of party control		
	1977-81	1981-85	1985-89
Total expenditure per unit of 'assessed need' (2)	+0.71	+0.23	+0.22
Personal Social Services:			
Spending per 'dependent' person (3)	+0.33	+0.66**	+0.75**
Fieldworkers per 'dependent' person	+0.41	+0.76**	+0.71**
Adminstrators per 'dependent' person	+0.80*	+0.64**	+0.68**
Spending per elderly person in residential care	-0.12	+0.35	+0.13
Home-help contact hours per elderly person	+0.92*	+0.79***	+0.93***

(b) Districts

	Periods of party control				
	1974-76	1976-79	1979-83	1983-87	1987-
Total expenditure per unit of 'assessed need'	-	-	+0.39*	+0.51***	+0.18
Housing:					
% new building by local council	+0.22**	+0.61***	+0.42***	+0.21*	+0.20
Sales per 1,000 houses (4)	-0.02	-0.39	-0.21	+0.07	+0.20
Ratio of rents to gross value (5)	+0.01	-0.17	-0.17	+0.14	+0.15
Rate fund subsidies	+0.08	+0.14	+0.22*	+0.29*	+0.04

Notes:
(1) The figures show the mean 'Z-score' for Labour-controlled authorities on each policy measure. A positive figure indicates that Labour councils are above average, and a negative figure indicates that Labour councils are below average. The following symbols indicate whether the Labour mean is significantly different from the non-Labour mean, using a one-tailed test:

* = 0.10
** = 0.05
*** = 0.01

The sample sizes vary, depending on data availability.

(2) Ratio of local expenditure to assessment of expenditure need by central government.

(3) The 'dependent' part of the population is measured as people under 16 plus people over retirement age. These groups are the primary clients of the personal social services.

(4) Most of the dwellings that have been sold are houses rather than flats. Therefore the number of houses is a more appropriate denominator than the total number of dwellings.

(5) Rents may be influenced not only by political ideology but also by the quality of dwellings. Gross value is a proxy for the standard of individual dwellings and the general quality of the neighbourhood.

Table 12: The extent of diversity in different policy areas

Size of coefficient	County boroughs and county councils of variation 1950s, 1960s, 1970s
0-0.05	Education: secondary pupil/teacher ratio
0.06-0.10	Education: spending per primary and secondary pupil; primary pupil/teacher ratio
0.11-0.15	Total spending; Education: total spending; Police: spending and officers
0.16-0.20	Education: primary, secondary and further spending. Library staff
0.21-0.25	PSS: spending on the elderly; Fire: spending and officers; Libraries: spending and books
0.26-0.30	PSS: spending on children's services and residential homes, spending per domestic help case
0.31-0.40	Housing: percentage new building by council
0.41-0.50	PSS: spending on children's homes and domestic help; Recreation: spending; Housing: rate fund subsidy; Highway: spending
0.51-0.60	Planning: spending
0.61-0.70	
0.71+	

Welsh counties, 1980s

Welsh districts 1980s

Education: secondary pupil/teacher ratio

Education: spending per primary and
secondary pupil; primary pupil/teacher ratio,
total spending. Total spending and staff.
Police: spending and officers; Fire: spending;
PSS: spending per elderly resident in care

Education: spending on books and equip-   Housing rents
ment per secondary pupil, nursery pupil/teacher
ratio; PSS: total spending

PSS: Fieldworkers and administrators;
Further education spending; Libraries:
 spending, staff, book issues; Police and
Fire civilians; Planning: spending

Total spending; Refuse collection spending

PSS: home-help contact hours per   Total full-time staff. Environmental health
elderly person   spending.Rate collection: spending and staff
                                              per hereditament

Fire: full-time staff; Transport: revenue   Refuse collection staff
support; Highways: total spending and
spending on non-principal roads

Highways: spending on principal roads   Total part-time staff. Refuse collection:
                                              spending per tonne; Recreation: spending
                                              and revenue/cost ratio; Trading services:
                                              revenue/cost ratio

                                              Refuse disposal: total spending, spending
                                              per tonne Planning: spending. Concessionary
                                              fares: spending

                                              Refuse disposal staff; Housing: sales and grants

Fire: part-time staff   Housing: new building and rate subsidy;
                                              Museums, theatres and galleries: spending

Note:

(1) All variables are per capita unless otherwise indicated

Source: Wales as Tables 3 to 10; County Boroughs and County Councils pre-1974 - derived
from data in Boaden (1970), Danziger (1978), Foster *et al* (1980), Sharpe and Newton (1984),
Coldsmith and Page (1987)

Table 13: Variations in financial delegation between authorities

	% of GSB held by LE	Mandatory Exceptions (percentages)	Discretionary (10% limit) (percentages)	(no limit)
	(1)	(2)	(3)	(4)
Clwyd	35.0	11.0	8.3	15.7
Dyfed	36.8	11.4	9.2	16.2
Gwent	34.4	13.2	9.1	12.1
Gwynedd	35.7	8.7	8.9	18.1
Mid-Glamorgan	33.7	10.9	10.0	12.8
Powys	32.7	9.0	9.9	13.8
South Glamorgan	28.9	10.5	9.5	8.9
West Glamorgan	31.1	13.3	8.7	9.1

Notes

Column (l) is the percentage of the General Schools Budget held back by the LEA

Column (2) covers expenditure that the LEA cannot delegate

Column (3) covers expenditure that is discretionery, subject to a 10 per cent limit

Column (4) covers expenditure that is discretionary but not subject to a 10 per cent limit

Source: adapted from Welsh Office Press Release, October 23 1990.
The details of these figuress have been disputed by LEAs.

APPENDIX 2: A REGRESSION MODEL OF COUNTIES' BLOCK GRANT RECEIPTS

$BGRANT = A + B_1 NEEDi + B_2 TBASEi + B_3 WALESi + Ei$

WHERE 'A' IS A CONSTANT, 'E' IS AN ERROR TERM, 'i' DENOTES AN INDIVIDUAL COUNCIL AND

BGRANT = BLOCK GRANT PER CAPITA

NEED = GRANT RELATED EXPENDITURE PER CAPITA

TBASE = RATEABLE VALUE PER CAPITA

WALES = A BINARY VARIABLE, CODED 1 FOR A WELSH COUNTY AND 0 FOR AN ENGLISH COUNTY

THE RESULTS OF TESTING THIS MODEL WERE :

BGRANT = 27.87
+0.90 NEED
[0.04]
-1.43 TBASE
[0.04]
+15.09 WALES
[2.69]
+ E   [STANDARD ERRORS IN BRACKETS]

R^2 = 0.99
F = 1694.26

ALL THREE EXPLANATORY VARIABLES AND THE R^2 ARE SIGNIFICANT AT 0.0000

APPENDIX 3: THE MAPPING EXERCISE

The general map

The map is intended to illustrate how local authorities fit in to the three 'ideal type' models explored in Part I. The map examines certain features of local government and shows how such features can be interpreted under different models.

	Enabler (market)	Traditional (direct provider)	Enabler (participatory)
Role emphasis	X Town Plc	Direct service provision	Community government
Role culture	Competitive	Reactive	Pro-active
Strategic planning	Parameters set by market	Scale and priorities by services	Response to community
Basis of service provision	Mixed economy	Professionally based	Variety of community provision
Basis of internal organisation	Contract specification negotiation	Service departments	Matrix, decentralised
Political management structures	Executive Management Board	Professionals as gatekeepers	Area committees
Accountability	Mutual responsibilities	Members and committees	To local people
Scope for discretion	By negotiation	Depends upon professional autonomy	High in response to local preferences
Basis of relations with other authorities	Ring holder	Self-sufficient	Strong commitment
Basis of relations with other bodies	Ring holder	Self-sufficient	Strong commitment to local groups

The map for education

	Enabler (market)	Traditional (direct provider)	Enabler (participatory)
Role emphasis	Competitive; opting out	Direct services provision	Community education
Strategic management	Market	Determined by authority	Partnerships
Discretion	Maximise market forces	Authority involvement	Autonomy of schools
Relations with other authorities	Limited	Self-sufficient	Networks
Service delivery	Agencies	Close control	New forms

The map for housing

	Enabler (market)	Traditional (direct provider)	Enabler (participatory)
Geographical location	Decentralised	Centralised	Decentralised
Internal organisation	Contract specification negotiation and management	Service departments	Decentralised
Organisational culture	Customer	Client	Citizen
Housing associations	Pro-active	Pragmatic	Pro-active but control market
Contracting-out	Pro-active	Reactive	Pro-active but control market
Content of service	Wide, in response to customer	Narrow definition	Wide, 'social- services-style'

MEMBERSHIP OF THE LOCAL AND CENTRAL GOVERNMENT RELATIONS RESEARCH COMMITTEE

Sir Charles Carter, FBA, Vice Chairman, Joseph Rowntree Foundation; President, Policy Studies Institute

Professor Alan Alexander, Scottish Local Authorities Management Centre

Roger Almond, IMI plc; CBI Local Government Committee

John Barratt, formerly Chief Executive, Cambridgeshire

Councillor Jeremy Beecham, leader, Newcastle Upon Tyne City Council; Vice-Chairman, Association of Metropolitan Authorities

Mrs Rita Hale, Chartered Institute of Public Finance and Accountancy

Sir Trevor Hughes, KCB, formerly Permanent Secretary, Welsh Office

Councillor Philip Mayo, formerly National Freight Consortium

Sir George Moseley, KCB, formerly Permanent Secretary, Department of the Environment

Sir Patrick Nairne, Trustee, Joseph Rowntree Foundation; formerly Permanent Secretary, Department of Health and Social Security and Master of St Catherine's College, Oxford

Anthony Prendergast, formerly Chair, Planning Committee, Westminster City Council

Mrs Muriel Pritchard, formerly Belfast City Council; Chair, Belfast Charitable Trust for Integrated Education

David Scott, Local Government Correspondent, *The Scotsman*

Dr John Sewel, Aberdeen University, formerly President, Convention of Scottish Local Authorities

Professor Ken Young, Queen Mary's and Westfield College, London